1917

Your Life God's Way

I dedicate this book to Dorinda Miller who has over the years been such an encouragement and inspiration, who supported me when things were not going well and gave me advice and wisdom when I didn't think I needed it!

Your Life God's Way

J. John

Marshall Pickering

Edited by Nicholas Aiken
Illustrated by Dan Donovan

Marshall Morgan and Scott
Marshall Pickering
3 Beggarwood Lane, Basingstoke, Hants RG23 7LP,
UK

First published in 1986 by Marshall Morgan and
Scott Publications Ltd
Part of the Marshall Pickering Holdings Group
A subsidiary of the Zondervan Corporation

ISBN 0 551 01346 X

Text Set in 10/11 Century by
Input Typesetting Ltd, London
Printed in Great Britain by
Anchor Brendon Ltd, Tiptree, Essex

Contents

Preface

This book is not meant to be a ladder of logic from one chapter to the next, but a kind of literary bouquet. You choose your flower and wear it that day. If it turns out to be a cactus . . . I did mean well.

No one book can do it all. But suppose you and I could spend a day together talking . . . what would I talk about? Difficulties in the Christian life, dryness, temptation, warnings about the use of our tongue, a little bit about the things we ought to be doing as Christians and a glimmer of heaven. That is what this book is about.

As always many people have shared in the writing of this book. Thanks to Debbie Thorpe and Christine Whitell my book editors. Particular thanks to Eric Delve who challenged and encouraged me in the Christian race (with tears of sorrow and many more of laughter). To Father Thomas of Mount Saint Bernard Abbey, my spiritual adviser. To Justin Fashanu, with whom all the ideas in this book were discussed at our early morning Bible studies. To our friends Nick and Sue Brotherwood, Gerald Barlow and Lois Thompson for honest talking. To Peggy Wright for constant prayer and to all those in our prayer group. To James Catford—a great source of information. To my colleague Brenda Thompson who read the manuscript and made helpful suggestions. I would also like to thank the Lord for two people (now in heaven) whose writings have had a great influence in my life, namely, St. Ignatius and Evelyn Underhill. Thanks to Lynn Irvine for all the typing. Last, but not least, to my wife Killy who read and re-read the manuscript and made our little home a peaceful place to write.

J. John
Nottingham
January 1986

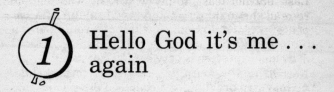

1 Hello God it's me . . . again

Problem situation

I want to know what to do to get back to God. I've been out of His plans for a while. Okay, I've been backsliding!

Do you think God will have me back? It's been a while. Even your best friends get sick of you if you always let them down—does God?

State of affairs

- —I've got lost
- —I've given up on prayer
- —and on Church
- —I'm depressed spiritually
- —I feel bad
- —What do I do?

Well!

1. Going back to God
I know I've got to get back to God. I know. Back to

God . . . from where? No doubt from a hundred and one different situations, alley-ways, hangups and wrong turns.

Maybe it has just happened without you really deciding to go against God. (Or maybe you did.) You haven't really got involved in bad or unchristian things, but you haven't been asking what's right and wrong any more. You're not praying and not paying attention to God. Now if that's you, then you are *backsliding*.

The whole process is very subtle. Not many people wake up in the morning and decide to backslide. You just stop praying for a couple of days. On a cold Sunday morning you stay in bed a bit longer and out goes the morning service from your routine. Only for this week you reassure yourself, but one plus one plus one . . . and the pile soon starts to grow awfully big. If it isn't dealt with then it's easy to become unfaithful in bigger things, or unreliable maybe and possibly critical of other Christians (particularly the ones who tell you to shape up). No doubt if that is you—the real problem is that you feel trapped. And no doubt it feels as though there is a plot to keep you trapped where you are because you have distanced yourself from God.

Most people are not very good at forgiving (that's not an excuse), but if you have hurt someone and you sincerely want to apologise and ask for forgiveness, sometimes they are the ones who actually hold out. They can give the impression that they are distant from you and very cold, and so when you pluck up the courage to say 'sorry' they get all steamed up and annoyed. 'You're *sorry* are you? It's a fat lot of good to be sorry *now*—you should have thought of that before,' or, 'You've got a nerve showing your face around here!' Because some of your past attempts at apologising may be filled with

2

painful memories you reckon that God must also react like that. Maybe God is going to say to you, 'You've got some nerve coming back now, after all the messing about you've done'. It's then when some people make a big mistake by trying (as we say in Christian language) to sort it out in our own strength. This simply doesn't work. You try to look decent enough to ask for help and forgiveness. But it's a bit like trying to get totally clean so you look nice enough to take a shower. Or like saying that you are far too sick to visit the doctor, so you've got to sort yourself out first and when you are looking better you'll go and visit him. It's ridiculous.

Character File

Failure Cases

Peter — Big-mouth disciple who said 'No' to Jesus.

Mary Magdalene — She was bad!!

3

In the Gospels we read many times of the people who criticised Jesus because He was hanging around with the riff-raff. In Matthew Chapter 9: 9, Jesus was having dinner at Matthew's house and Matthew's former associates were also there, people who were living against God's will. To those who criticised Jesus because He was friendly with 'sinners', He said that His ministry was needed by sinners, just as doctor's services are needed by the sick.

In recent years I have been a fan of a local football team. Have you noticed (if you are a supporter) that when your team loses the first ten matches of the season—it's not really a great feeling? I've been into the players' lounge after a game they have lost and they look gloomy and depressed, and when that continues to happen, the players, as individuals and as a team, find it really hard to generate enthusiasm and to be positive for the rest of the season. Instead of looking forward to a win next time, they go on to the field or the court hoping that they won't get wiped out again.

Maybe something similar has happened in your relationship with God, and you just feel that you are a loser. No go. You've tried but it just hasn't worked. You're not cut out to be a Christian. What about the individuals in the Bible—were they cut out for it? St. Peter was always ready to say that he would follow Jesus to the bitter end, but when the crunch came, Peter denied Jesus. Mary Magdalene, an ex-prostitute, even if she was 'ex' would not have been considered the Christian type. And the Saints? They are now, but were they always? Of course not. When Jesus looks at you, He sees you as you are and all that you have done and yet He accepts you if you are willing to build your life on Him. And if He can accept Peter, Matthew, Mary

4

Magdalene and transform them, then what is there that He cannot do with you, if you only allow Him?

Maybe you are saying 'I *do* want to get back with God and I *don't* want to get back with God'. Your head tells you that your life will be far better and more peaceful if you do return to God, but your heart or your habits make you question this. 'It will be far too hard', you tell yourself. You realise you are going to have to change and so you conclude it might be better just to let things be. Well, if that is the case, then do pray and pray as honestly as you can. Tell Him exactly how you feel, 'Lord I do want to come back yet I don't want to, please speak to me.' Maybe you have to pray this over and over again. But remember this, He is waiting for you to come back, so don't worry what other people think of you or what they will say. Tell Him that you know you have strayed, that you really want to be forgiven, and that you do want to be friends again, and that you do want Him to fill your life with His Holy Spirit so that you can begin to walk with Him again. And while you are praying, think of the story of the Prodigal Son or maybe we should call it the story of the Loving Father who wept with joy when he saw his son and ran to meet him. Now if this has spoken to you either re-read this chapter, or read the next one and then re-read this one, and then pray!

Scripture Spotlight

'I will never turn away anyone who comes to me.'
John 6: 37
'But because of your great love I can come into your house, I can worship in your holy temple.'
Psalm 5: 7
'I will forgive their sins and will no longer remember their wrongs.' Hebrews 8: 12

Action response.

—Identify the situation you are in (by reading this book you're half way to that).
—Go and talk to someone, a Christian leader or Christian friend.
—Tell God how you really feel.
—Set yourself a few simple objectives like praying for five minutes each day or doing one thing for God every day.

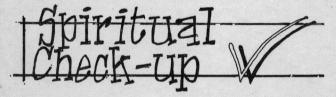

Spiritual Check-up ✓

How did you get out of this situation before?

'When prodigals return
great things are done.'
A.A. Dowty.

2 How much do you think you are worth?

Jesus told us, 'Love your neighbour as *yourself*' and yet so many Christians have such a low self-image, how *do* they begin to love their neighbours? Jesus told us we should be patient with our neighbours, kind, gentle and forgiving. Yet some people destroy themselves with self-hatred. They don't forgive themselves, they hold grudges against themselves and remain angry with themselves. Now let's get one thing clear, doing this is not humility! One aspect of humility is truth and the truth is that we (you and me) are loved and lovable because God, by loving us first, made us that way. Sometimes we call our 'putting ourselves down'—particularly after a sin—an expression of remorse. But putting oneself down is rejecting God's love and thereby cutting off the source from which we receive our power to love. Do you feel like this, pretty worthless, and so far, has this book only made you feel worse? (I'm sorry if it has, but here are some thoughts.) A low self-image may be the result of an overweight or an underweight condition, failure to achieve, loneliness or an inability to make friends, a physical handicap, too short, too tall or maybe all of these put together!

I met a girl recently who had a low self-image because her breasts were so big (others no doubt because theirs are too small).

First, Jesus Christ thinks so much of you that He is preparing a great house for you in heaven. Before He made His final preparations to die on the Cross, rise from the dead and return to heaven, He gave this promise. 'I go to prepare a place for you.' John 14: 2. And what a home it will be, built personally by the Carpenter of Nazareth. There's an interesting story in the Old Testament about what King David did for a man whose name was Mephibosheth. In the Hebrew his name means 'breathing shame'. What a reason for a low self-image! He also had another reason. As a child he had a bad accident which left him 'lame on his feet' (Samuel 9: 3). Also Mephibosheth lived in a miserable, out-of-the-way place, called Lodebar (verse 4). But all this was before King David came into the picture.

David heard about Mephibosheth who was his old friend Jonathan's son. He had been hiding from David because he thought that David might want to kill him so that he wouldn't be around to claim the throne as King Saul's grandson.

David sent for him and when Mephibosheth entered the palace he showed just how low an opinion of himself he had. He called himself 'a dead dog' (verse 8). But David set a high value on Mephibosheth. He gave him land and servants, a free meal ticket to eat at the King's table as one of the King's sons and said in effect 'Mephibosheth, you're moving in with me. My home, the palace, is your home!'

What David did for Mephibosheth gives us a little understanding of what Jesus has done for us. That should begin to help us set the proper value on ourselves. If he accepts us then we should accept ourselves. Also Jesus himself will someday come to

9

receive us. David sent for Mephibosheth, and the son of David, our Lord Jesus Christ, will come in person for us. Jesus Christ has placed such a high value on us.

Scripture Spotlight

'As high as the sky is above the earth
   so great is His love for those who honour Him.
As far as the East is from the West
   so far does He remove our sins from us.'

Psalm 103: 12, 13.

'But you are the chosen race, the King's priests, the holy nation, God's own people, chosen to proclaim the wonderful acts of God; who called you out of darkness into His own marvellous light. At one time you were not God's people, but now you are His people. At one time you did not know God's mercy, but now you have received His mercy.'

1 Peter 2: 9, 10.

How do you feel?

Maybe it's things in your past that have caused you to feel the way you do, and in spite of all that has been said in this chapter you still feel it hasn't helped. Maybe when you were born you were not loved and all through your childhood you felt that your parents did not want you. There was always an 'if' to their love. 'You are very bad if you make finger prints on the wall.' 'If you want mummy and daddy really to love you, then get an 'A' in your report from school,' and so on. These things are conveying the idea that you are good, worthwhile, loved and lovable only if ... and if ... and if you do something, avoid something or become something. Some parents are at fault by using love as a reward, by turning off love as a punishment, by holding grudges and constantly reminding a child of past failings.

Another form of love which is perhaps more harmful is the forcefully dominating and demanding type. In this case your parents (one or both) love you because they need you, because they are actually starving for love themselves, maybe due to their own emotional insecurity. The parents 'over-love' and do everything to win your love by keeping you dependent, to the extent that you do not mature to your full potential. You do not feel loved for your own sake but because your parents need you simply as a means to satisfy their own craving to love and to be loved. You end up going through life insisting that you were always loved by your parents while at the same time you feel unloved.

The human heart cannot go long with the condition of not being loved. A continuous experience of feeling unloved and therefore being unable to love oneself can cause worry, frustration and fear because God put in us an unquenchable desire to love and to be loved.

I've only outlined two possible root causes, maybe you suffer from one of these or maybe there are other causes. Whatever the cause, God can heal and restore and renew you. Ask Him to heal your past, tell Him your deepest needs, share with Him your deepest feelings, invite the Holy Spirit to fill your heart (and it may also be good to speak to an older Christian as well).

My prayer for you if this applies to you is that you may soak up the love of Christ. Then you can go through life knowing that He loves you and you are worthy of His love and have the strength to share that love with others. There are many Psalms that describe our deepest human needs. Read some of them. Especially look at Psalm 51 or Psalm 102.

Scripture Spotlight

'But the people of Jerusalem said, "The Lord has abandoned us! He has forgotten us."
So the Lord answers,
"Can a woman forget her own baby and not love the child she bore?
Even if a mother should forget her child, I will never forget you." '

Isaiah 49:14, 15.

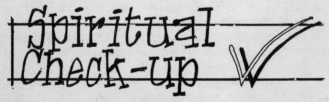

Spiritual Check-up ✔

List things that you feel about yourself at the moment. Then list things from what you have read that God feels about you. How do they compare?

'The holiness of God
excuses no sin, but
the love of God
forgives all sin
through Christ.'

Anonymous

3 A new allegiance

'Therefore, if anyone is in Christ, he is a new creation, the old has gone, the new has come.'

2 Corinthians 5: 17.

Some of us look back with great joy when we remember the day we turned to Christ and began a new life with Him. For some of us, this was a sudden event; but for others it may be different. Not all conversions or coming to Christ are sudden and clear cut. We are all individuals and we all possess different temperaments; that's why the Bible is filled with so many varying incidents of people meeting Christ. Each is described uniquely (the language used is peculiar to each person!), and the path leading up to this point no doubt for many of them was very long and perhaps winding.

Some of you may feel you don't fit in the above bracket, you don't have any memory of a spiritual encounter, conversion . . . that does not mean you must doubt your relationship with Christ. Just because you can't look back to a definite date when you made a conscious decision does not mean you are not a Christian. Maybe you were brought up in a Christian home and you cannot remember a time when you were not a Christian.

The term conversion really means turning round and refers to the time in a person's life when they are directed to God, when they pass from a position of spiritual death to spiritual life.

'I tell you the truth, unless you turn and become like little children, you will never enter the Kingdom of God.'   Matthew 18: 3

The name 'Christian' was first given to those disciples in Antioch who believed and turned to the Lord (Acts 11: 21, 26). A Christian, then, in the Biblical sense, is someone who has handed himself over to Jesus Christ and follows His direction, and has therefore turned away from the path he was originally walking. The important thing to understand about coming to know Christ—no matter what phraseology is used to describe it—a definite link between us and God is made!

15

In order for us to live the Christian life it must be understood what 'becoming a Christian' involves. Whether we can remember or not the moment of turning, *there need be no doubt about one's actual position now.*

Let's recap

The Bible says that sin separates us from God. Sin means failing to do what God has commanded us to do and trespass means doing what has been forbidden for us to do. Because of this there is a barrier between us and God (we put the barrier up!). The consequence of all this is death, *but* Jesus Christ came into the world to give us forgiveness and life. 'God has given us eternal life and this life is in His Son. He who has the Son has life, he who does not have the Son of God does not have Life.' (1 John 5: 11, 12)

In the animal world, life is created as soon as conception takes place. In the spiritual world, eternal life begins whenever anyone, believing in Jesus Christ, receives His new life and so is 'born again'. It is God's Holy Spirit entering our lives that makes us a child of God.

This is not just turning a new leaf, or a moral clean-up, but a new life—God's life entering us. It is important to realise God's initiative in all this and how much it cost:

'God demonstrates His own love for us in that while we were still sinners Christ died for us.'

Romans 5: 8

After the new birth has taken place, there is often a great sense of peace of mind and heart. The important thing if you are a new Christian, or have

16

just come back to the Lord, is to persevere and build on the truths you know about God. The reliable facts of God's word will in time be borne out in your personal experience, and you will progress in your Christian growth and maturity. So don't look back, look forward. If you are still doubting that you have ever come to Christ then pray now:

Lord Jesus, I turn to you.
Thank you for dying for me.
I ask you to forgive me
    and invite you to come into my
    life now.
Thank you for answering this prayer.

Wise Words

'Conversion is no repairing of the old building; but it takes all down and erects a new structure. The sincere Christian is quite a new fabric, from the foundation to the roof all is new.'
Joseph Alleine

Keeping the relationship going

Our Lord wants us to be in fellowship with Him. He longs for us to have a confident friendship with Him. The key to this is what is called *Prayer*. This can be difficult, but there is nothing so essential as time alone with the Lord. It is this time spent with Him that brings growth in the Christian life. Prayer gives us depth. Out of prayer flows God's power into our lives and through our lives to others. Yes, I know we are all busy! But when we are busy do we miss our meals? Of course not—however busy we are we still eat, because we need food to grow. Similarly with prayer ... we *need* to spend time with the Lord to grow as His children.

The disciples of Jesus asked Him how they should pray and Jesus said,

'This is how you should pray,
Our Father in heaven
hallowed be your name
your Kingdom come
your will be done
On earth as it is in heaven.
Give us today our daily bread
Forgive us our sins

as we forgive those who have sinned against us.
And lead us not into temptation
but deliver us from the evil one.'

Matthew 6: 9

Jesus was saying, 'This is how you should pray.' He didn't say this is the prayer to pray. So He probably meant us to look at the structure of this prayer and copy it when we pray. Let's look at the prayer Jesus prayed. The first three statements are all concerned with God and *His glory*. I always start any prayer time with the Lord by worshipping Him, acknowledging who He is and praising Him with all that I am for all that He is. I thank Him for answered prayer, for what He is doing and for His love.

If you are praying to Him and are conscious of sin, then confess the sin to Him and claim cleansing and forgiveness through the blood of our Lord Jesus Christ.

'If we confess our sins, He is faithful and just and will forgive us our sins and purify us from all unrighteousness.'

1 John 1: 9

Tell the Lord what has happened, acknowledge that you may have hurt Him, yourself or someone else and ask for forgiveness. Believe that He has given it and spend some time thanking Him for His forgiveness; you could use the Psalms for this relating your own experiences as you read them. Remember Psalm 51!

The next part of Jesus' prayer is, 'Give us today our daily bread'—pray for God's *goodness* to be shown in your daily needs. Think through the day and ask God to provide for you where necessary. Prayer changes things. It is sometimes useful to keep some prayer lists on which names and requests can be written down and regularly mentioned.

The next phrase of the Lord's prayer then says, 'Forgive us our sins', asking for God's *grace* to be given. Any crisis you are facing in your life, any hurdles you will come across today, people you find difficult—ask God for His grace to be given to you to discover His strength and peace to deal with all of these things. *There is no substitute for time with the Lord.* You want power in your life? Then time with the Lord is the key.

'Call to me and I will answer you and tell you great and unsearchable things you do not know.'

Jeremiah 33: 3

'So I say to you—Ask and it will be given to you. Seek and you will find. Knock and the door will be opened to you. For everyone who asks receives, He who seeks finds, and to him who knocks the door will be opened.'

Luke 11: 9 – 10

'I prayed to the God of heaven.'

Nehemiah 2: 4

What if our thoughts wander while we are talking to the Lord and we find it hard to concentrate? First, start your time with the Lord by reading His word. This directs our thoughts on to the King's business. Secondly, I find praying aloud very helpful—it helps me concentrate better. I don't always pray out loud of course, but also in silence, and sometimes I can just sit and ponder over Scripture for half an hour which inspires me to talk to the Lord. If I find that my mind is distracted, let's say by two people talking nearby, realise that they are not the problem. What do you do about the situation? You have three options: either to fight it and say, 'I'm *not* going to listen (then the situation becomes worse!), or to listen in (!), or do the right thing and tell the Lord you are sorry you have wandered and ask for His help as you talk to Him despite all the distractions.

It is also very important to become familiar with the Lord's word, the Bible. But as with eating, it is better to take a little in at a time, digesting it before going on. Get to know the New Testament first; read a passage and keep reading it till something strikes you, then pause and think about what you have read, whether it be a passage, a verse or even one word. Ask the Holy Spirit to teach you its meaning and to help you receive what He wants you to learn, and thank Him when He does.

When you are next together with your Bible Study group you might find it helpful to discuss these questions:

Where do you find is the best place to pray?

How long should you pray for?

Should you only pray when you feel like it?

How does prayer help you?

Have you experienced any answers to prayer recently?

Wise Words

'Prayer does not change God, but changes him who prays.'

Sören Kierkegaard

'The most important thing in any prayer is not what we say to God, but what God says to us. We often pray and then hurry away without giving God a chance to answer.'

from a Christian newspaper

'If Christians spent as much time praying as they do grumbling, they would soon have nothing to grumble about.'

Anonymous

'Prayer is conversation with God.'

Clement of Alexandria

'God's road map—the Bible.'

Kenyon A. Palmer.

5 Spiritual depression

Everyone who is a Christian goes through times of spiritual depression. You feel as if God is miles away and has given up on you.

Are you spiritually depressed at the moment or have you been recently? If you have, which of the below applied to you at the time?

(a) School or work was not going well   —
(b) You had an argument in your family   —

(c) Your girl friend/boy friend chucked you   —
(d) Someone upset you by something they
     did or said   —
(e) You felt lost   —
(f) Prayer felt like a waste of time   —
(g) Church was boring   —
(h) Your relationship with God seemed
     to have collapsed   —
(i) You felt rejected   —

If you ticked all or one of a—d, then probably part
of your spiritual depression was due to a rough situation that was getting you down. If you have ticked
one or all of e—i, then read on because we are going
to get to the bottom of this, and see if we can come
up with some answers.

But before we go on remember every Christian
goes through times of depression, you are not the
only one. This experience is not necessarily a sign
that the Lord is displeased with us, or that we have
somehow been negligent in our commitment to Him.

Analysis

*Three possible reasons why we suffer spiritual
depression:*

1. It is a trial period *allowed* by God so we can
be tested as to whether we love God or just
love His gifts; whether we will continue to
follow His call in bad times as well as in
good times.
2. It is a time when God lets us experience
our own poverty and need, and gives us
an opportunity to grow in true humility,
realising how empty we are.
3. Perhaps it is our own fault (if we have

24

consciously gone against God), or perhaps are shallow in our walk with the Lord, and so the enemy plays on this superficiality.

It is important, if you are feeling more spiritually dead than alive, that you consider the following four guidelines:

1. Do not make any important decisions while you are feeling like this, or change previous decisions. Hold on to any decision you felt guided to make before this period.

2. Resist the temptation just to sit back and do nothing, hoping that your feelings will blow over. Try to pray more. Telling God how awful you feel is better than not talking to Him at all.

3. Sometimes, with spiritual depression, we feel that God has left us. By *faith* we *know* that He is always with us in the strength and power of His grace, but at the time of apparent abandonment we are little aware of His care and concern. We experience neither the support nor the sweetness of His love. Have faith enough to *trust* Him. At least *Try*.

4. The important attitude to nourish at such a time is patience. It won't last for ever. Patience can ease the frustration, dryness or emptiness and so allow us to live through it a little less painfully.

During this time the enemy will try to make you impatient and try to stop you praying. It is important that you understand his tactics and do the opposite. So, if you normally pray for ten minutes a day, then pray for fifteen minutes. Do the opposite from what the Devil inspires. If the Devil's tactics succeed once in your life, he'll be back to do more damage. If he can reduce your ten minutes of prayer to five, he'll soon whittle it down to nothing. But if you prayed more, then the Devil would quickly abandon this line of attack. No one has ever accused the Devil of being stupid . . . disobedient, yes, but definitely not stupid!

Trust that God's grace and help are present even though you may not feel Him near. You will not always feel deserted as you do now. It is easy to be spiritually paralysed by an experience of depression, but you must work to prevent this.

Before looking again at the three reasons for spiritual depression, let us look at the story of Job. The unknown author clearly identifies with Job in his debate against God.

'One day the angels came to present themselves before the Lord and Satan also came with them. The Lord said to Satan, "Where have you come from?" Satan answered the Lord, "From roaming through the earth and going to and fro in it." Then the Lord said to Satan, "Have you considered my servant Job? There is no one on earth like him; he is blameless and upright, a man who fears God and shuns evil." "Does Job fear God for nothing?" Satan replied, "Have you not put a hedge around him and his household and everything he has? You have blessed the work of his hands, so that his flocks and herds are spread throughout the land. But stretch out your hand and strike everything he has, and he will surely curse you to your face." The Lord said to Satan, "Very well, then, everything he has is in your hands, but on the man himself do not lay a finger.'

Job 1: 6 – 12

26

Satan, with the permission of the Lord God, then went out to strike down Job's livestock, his servants and even his children. And when these tragedies failed to shake Job's trust, Satan returned to ask the Lord for permission to hurt him directly.

"Skin for skin!" Satan replied, "A man will give all he has for his own life. But stretch out your hand and strike his flesh and bones and he will surely curse you to your face." The Lord said to Satan, "Very well, then, he is in your hands, but you must spare his life."

Job 2: 4 – 6

The important insight here is that Satan is the *cause* of Job's terrible experiences, though he cannot act without God's permission. And why does God permit Satan to try Job so severely? In some mysterious way, it is to test Job's love and faithfulness.

So now back to the three possible reasons for spiritual depression:

1. God's desire to test our love (as in Job's life).
2. An opportunity for us to grow in humility, that we may arrive at that place of utter dependence upon Him.
3. Our own negligence.

When I talk to people who feel dried up, they nearly all think that they must have displeased God in some way, and that it is their own fault that the Lord seems far away. This, as we have seen, is one possibility, but it is not the only one. I find that those who take their relationship with the Lord seriously are more likely to feel that depression is a sign of their own negligence. *Even if this is true, the depression is not intended to punish them but to wake them up to the fact they have drifted.* We can drift even unconsciously. The pressure of work can lead us to neglect our prayer; maybe some friendships make us compromise our commitment to the Lord, or we have absorbed worldly values without realising it. In all these cases and others, the Lord may permit the Devil to do his work, but while the Devil's goal is to destroy the person, the Lord's intent is to make them aware of what is happening and to restore them. Spiritual depression can be a flashing red light warning us of the danger of the state we are in.

Some Christians will say, 'I can't see what wrong I have done. When I look at my life it seems to me I fail in many ways, but I failed in the same ways in the past and then God seemed very close.' If this is the case, then we can be quite sure that negligence is not the reason for it.

'But', others may say, 'perhaps I have displeased the Lord in some way which I do not realise.' If they say this, I always insist that such doubts or fears should *not* be taken seriously. God is not playing guessing games with us! If we are in this situation, we should pray:

'Lord you know I want to please you. You are free to correct me in any way you desire. But at this moment I cannot see where I have gone wrong, so please make it clear to me, if I am somehow failing you. Unless or until you do, I will not take seriously these doubts.'

This is a good prayer to pray (if you can pray it honestly) as it is a strong affirmation of our trust in the Lord's goodness.

And, as we have said, there are two other reasons why we are experiencing depression. If we cannot pinpoint any specific negligence as its cause, we should look at the other two reasons.

It may be that you are being tested, to see how much you will advance despite your feelings. This whole area of testing (I must admit) puzzled me for many years because God knows everything about us, and I wondered why He needed to examine us. Then one day, when I was working in Northern Ireland, I realised that being tested is not intended to prove something to God but to show me my limitations, when left without signs of God in my life. It humbles us to realise that it is God we need and nothing else.

There is a good example of this in the manufacture of steel: Steel is an alloy of carbon and iron, and the process of refining and purifying the alloy is called 'testing'. To test the steel it is put under intense heat. Our difficult experience is probably a purifying fire in which our love is made strong and purer. It 'burns out' of us all the impurities of selfishness and arrogance, and it 'fuses' us to the Holy Spirit, just as the carbon and iron are fused together. If our lives were all bubbles and joys and swinging from chandeliers (as Eric Delve would put it), we would be soft and weak in our love.

Marriage also illustrates this. The couple being married say, 'for better or worse.' We think this means 'I hope it will always be better (and richer!) but if the worse does come I will try to persevere.' But that is not really the meaning of the phrase. I can't say I'm an expert on this; I've been married for three years and I'm still learning! But even in this short time I've realised that we need the 'worse' just as much as the 'better', strange as that may sound in an age of sentimentalised love. In the 'better' we learn the joy of loving, and in the 'worse' we learn to love unselfishly. The worse is the fire which purifies our love of all the self-seeking which is in each of us. It is when misunderstandings arise in marriage, when one person is disappointed by the other, that the real strength of love emerges. If they remain loyal to each other when things are difficult between them, then they can be sure they really love each other 'for better or worse' and not merely for what they get out of each other. Similarly, spiritual depression is the 'worse' of our love relationship with God. It both reveals and strengthens our love, it 'tests' that love in a purifying and transforming fire.

If we are going through depression the better we understand the experience, the better able we are to cope with it. Try to determine whether your experience is caused by 'negligence' or 'testing' or 'letting go' (being stripped of everything, so that you may embrace God fully and without hindrance). Perhaps a combination of these things is at work in you.

When you are in it, spiritual depression may seem like a long, a never-ending tunnel. Trust and persevere. God will console you and will bring you through it, and there is likely to be an afterglow too.

'For those who love God, all things work together for good.'

Romans 8: 28

. . . even spiritual depression!

30

Scripture Spotlight

'The sacrifice of God is a broken spirit: a broken and contrite heart He will not despise.'

Psalm 51: 17

'Blessed are the poor in spirit, for theirs is the Kingdom of Heaven.'

Matthew 5: 3

Wise Words

'The devil does not tempt unbelievers and sinners who are already his own.'

Thomas à Kempis

'Troubles are often the tools by which God fashions us for better things.'

Henry Ward Beecher

'Every time trouble comes, consider that through it the Lord is giving you a much needed lesson.'

Anon.

Spiritual Check-up ✓

'When you have been through difficult times before did you learn anything from them, or did any good come out of them for you?'

6 How to pray when it's the last thing you feel like doing

Rupert has a thumping headache, a temperature, a sore throat, sore eyes and aches all over. Someone offers Rupert some medicine. It's very good and it's even guaranteed to soothe him and ease his symptoms. It doesn't really taste that bad, in fact after the first swallow it's quite nice. And it is exactly what Rupert needs right at this moment. His aches and pains are getting worse, he's feeling very sorry for himself, and he's sure that the medicine is going to taste awful. He rolls his eyes into his head and makes a face at the thought of it. He is positive he won't be able to swallow a drop of it; besides, he says it probably won't do him any good anyway. It might work for some people but definitely not for him. Don't you think that Rupert is being a little dumb? He is turning away from something his body needs.

Excuses

We are always giving excuses to turn away from or refuse to consider the very thing we need most. Take, for example, someone who is pretty fit and has a good physical shape. That person really enjoys exercise. Take someone else who isn't fit at all and is a bit flabby. He or she needs the exercise, but . . . oh well . . . it's just so hard getting started. And such a person can dream up any number of excuses to avoid making that start. 'I'm going to feel pretty bad puffing, running around when I haven't even walked to the post box lately. I won't be any good at it. I'll just look stupid—anyhow I don't even have a tracksuit and what will the neighbours say!'

'It's going to take a long time before I see any results. I don't know whether I can take that. I'm the kind of person that needs results *now* (well, yesterday would be even better) and if I don't get them the way I want them I get so easily discouraged that I end up quitting and wonder why on earth I ever started.'

'Anyhow, why are we talking about all this? I'm probably too far gone anyway. I could do all the exercise in the world and still not get back in shape (well, I'm not sure if I ever was); I may as well live with what I've got.'

Believe it or not, it's just like that with praying. Just when talking with God is what we need most, it seems to be the most difficult, far-out, even dumb thing to do. And we use all sorts of excuses to avoid it or postpone it till we can avoid it altogether. Let's look at some of the situations where this happens.

'I've hurt God, and I know I have, because I have consciously broken His rules.'

You imagine that God is a revenge-minded person whose rules you have broken, or whom you have hurt. So you are really quite unsure about approaching Him; you are not sure about yourself, you feel bad and you are not sure what God thinks of you. If you do talk to Him you think He'll probably shout at you or sulk and make you feel even more guilty. So you think the answer is a cooling off period . . . Just let things wind down. You figure that probably after a few days or weeks God will have mellowed a bit and will probably have forgotten what you did. So, in the meantime, the best thing is probably for you to straighten up your act enough just to face Him.

Or maybe you feel you have let things go cold for a bit too long; you just haven't been around. This is not to say that you've committed a really terrible sin but, simply, you've been far from God and have separated yourself from Him and forsaken Him for a while. God is really quite close to zero in your life. A very uncomfortable situation you're in. You feel as you would in regards to a friend who has been really loyal to you but whom you've ignored and avoided for no good reason, and you can hear them saying as you approach them, 'You dirty dog, you've got a lot of nerve coming back after all this time and expecting things to be the same.'

So now you are just waiting around even though contact with God *now* is really what you need. From God's point of view it's never too late, but if you hang around too long, you may eventually convince yourself that it *is* too late and decide that your faith is really a lost cause—like the person who reckons he is so out of shape there really is no point even starting to exercise.

So what do we do if we feel like this—confused, ashamed and embarrassed? The danger is that you are moving towards the concrete stage 'thoroughly mixed up and set'—and you really don't want to do that! O.K. just go and make yourself a cup of coffee (or fruit juice) and come and sit back down and we'll go over this once again. The first thing to do is to take off any masks you may have on, take off the outer screen (cringe!). Just scrap the cover-up! There is a word in the Bible called 'guile', that means 'projecting what is false' and we tend to do that so regularly that sometimes we don't know that we are doing it. But listen here—you can't deceive God and you can't deceive yourself. God is the one person you don't have to play games with. He's got you pretty well worked out and in fact He knows the things about you which even you don't know! Now that might sound frightening in one way, but in another it's really quite comforting—for example, if you really do have some problem about your faith, you don't actually have to go to a court with God in order to convince Him about the way you feel.

With God you don't have to go miles and miles through diversions before you get to what you want to say. Just tell Him, 'God, Father, Lord, I've really done it this time—and I am really quite sad and very confused, and I don't know what to do, and I've got a feeling that it is going to happen again.'

Be honest

Honesty is the first step in dealing with all this, and you will find that you begin to feel a little better already. (Smile! It won't hurt.) With a friend whom you have ignored, you might not be sure what kind of a reception you will get when you try to re-establish connection. With God, does He get really angry with you, shout at you till you cry, then beat you black and blue and demand an explanation, then tell you He's going to ruin your life? . . . *Of course not!!* Don't you know the Prodigal Son story? Why don't we just pause and look. It's in Luke 15: 11 – 32.

This story is about a young person who turns away from God, forsaking Him to follow his own path where he expects to find excitement which will fulfil him. It also describes the progress—slow at first—which eventually brings him back, broken-hearted, to his Father's house.

The father has two sons. The younger son puts in a claim to his father for his share of the family inheritance. This is the beginning of the story. The words used are quite strong—let's see what they really mean 'Father *give me* . . .' This basically means, 'give me here and now what is going to be mine anyway when you are dead, but I can't wait till then, I want to live my own life now. You are really in my way, and as I'm impatient and can't wait for you to die, can you move out of my way? I don't want you running my life for me any more. I don't need a father. What I want is freedom and all the fruit of your life and labours to enjoy it. Step aside and let me go.' Such rebellion, in a nutshell, is *sin*. This summary of the son's attitude sounds quite cruel, yet don't we claim from God all He can give us—health, strength, success, all that we can be and all that we can have—to take it from Him and squander it, leaving him utterly forgotten and forsaken? It's like murdering God, behaving as though God was there for no other purpose than to toil and give us the fruits of His life, Himself of no ultimate significance for us.

The story progresses. Once in possession of all the wealth that the 'death' of his father gave him, the young man leaves the security of his home and goes his own way. The past is no more. Only the present exists.

Instantly popular, he is at the centre of every-thing. He imagines that it is to him that his new friends cling, but in fact he is being treated the same way he treated his father: he exists for his friends only because he is rich and can satisfy their demands.

He eats, drinks and is merry. Then comes the time when his wealth runs out and all is gone, even his friends betray him—he has nothing left but himself. He is cold. He has been rejected just as he rejected his father, but he faces an infinitely greater misery—his inward nothingness.

He needs food, so he has to work and the only job he can find is to feed pigs. This job at that time for the Jews was awful. Pigs were a symbol of impurity. Abandoned by all his friends, rejected on all sides, he stands face to face with himself and for the first time really looks at his life.

And then he remembers his father. Verse 17 says, 'at last he came to his senses.' The Prodigal Son goes home because the memory of his father gives him courage to return.

'So he got up and started back to his father. He was still a long way from home when his father saw him, he ran to his son and filled with compassion threw his arms around him and kissed him.'   (verse 20)

Don't you think that is amazing? The father immediately welcomes him and says to the servants, 'Quick! Bring the best robe and put it on him. Put a ring on his finger and sandals on his feet. Bring the fattened calf and kill it. Let's have a feast and celebrate. For this son of mine was dead and is alive again, he was lost and is found.'

Headlines . . . Son accepted back unconditionally!

The father doesn't say, 'When you have told me the

whole story—I'll see whether I can trust you again.'
No, his son's rags are thrown away and he is dressed
like a celebrity. The type of ring he was given
contained a seal that guaranteed any document. To
give one's ring to somebody meant trusting that
person with one's life, possessions, family
honour—everything. So if the Prodigal Son who
strayed could return to a lavish welcome can we if
we have strayed?

There are other things we can learn from this
story too. The other son appears on the scene, the
son who has always been a good worker in his
father's house, and leads a blameless life, but who
has never realised that the crucial factor in a father-
son relationship is not *work* but the *heart*, not *duty*
but *love*. He has been faithful in all things but he
has never been a true son except outwardly.

'Meanwhile the older son was in the field. When
he came near the house, he heard music and
dancing. So he called one of the servants and
asked him what was going on. "Your brother has
come," he replied, "and your father has killed the
fattened calf because he has him back safe and
sound." The older brother became angry and
refused to go in. So his father went out and
pleaded with him. But he answered his father,
"Look! All these years I've been slaving for you
and never disobeyed your orders. Yet you never
gave me even a young goat so I could celebrate
with my friends. But when this son of yours who
has squandered your property with prostitutes
comes home, you kill the fattened calf." "My son,"
the father said, "you are always with me and
everything I have is yours. But we had to
celebrate and be glad, because this brother of
yours was dead and is alive again, he was lost
and is found.'   (verse 25)

The reaction of the older son was to be jealous and disgusted. He was bitter over what he regarded as an injustice. A modern translation would be 'See here! I have been slaving for you all these years, and . . .' He speaks the language of self-pity.

By this parable as well as the two preceding this one in Luke 15, Jesus showed God's attitude towards sinners. He does not approve of their rebelliousness nor of their evil deeds, but He welcomes them back and restores them to favour when they repent.

It is a really wonderful freedom not to have to play a role or spend ages looking around for words and phrases to cover things up. With God you can be honest. Luke 15: 21 establishes the pattern, 'Father, I have sinned against heaven and against you.'

And if you feel that there is something that you are supposed to believe but that you have a real, honest difficulty with, tell God. Do you know anybody better equipped to help? What do you think He is going to do . . . strike you down with lightning for being honest? This, of course, assumes that you are being honest with Him. If you are trying to do a slick little number on God, perhaps to con Him into something, you will certainly find that it won't work, but if you are straight with God there is nothing He won't do to help you.

In Mark 9: 14, we read of a very distressed man who had a son with many problems. He came to Jesus but was not sure whether he could be helped or not. Did the man feel unworthy or did he doubt Jesus, or both? Whatever the case, Jesus did not exactly have your super-spiritual, super-faithful believer standing in front of Him. But the man talked honestly to Jesus. Did Jesus give up on him? No, of course not. He threw the man a challenge, not a rejection. The anguish that filled the father's heart is portrayed by his immediate response as he *cried out* almost in contradiction of himself. He did believe, and yet he was still very conscious of the unbelief that struggled with his desire to trust implicitly. His unbelief was not a refusal to believe, it was a weakness which the man could not deal with himself. Hence his cry to Jesus for help. A modern translation of what the man said could be, 'I do believe, well kind of, but not like I'm supposed to, I guess. Help me sort it all out.' Or as he was reported to have said 'I believe, help my unbelief.'

It is when praying may be the last thing you want to do, when praying may seem like a waste of time, that you have everything to gain by talking to Jesus.

In Matthew 18: 20 Jesus spoke about having faith as small as a mustard seed. Do you have faith as small as a mustard seed? (Go and buy some if you have never seen one before, they are tiny!) Jesus is saying if you have got faith only as big as a mustard seed it is enough. Just exercise it in a big God. When you exercise your muscles bulge, so when you flex your mustard seed faith, it will begin to grow and get stronger. Unbelief and prayerlessness are sure to result in spiritual powerlessness. The opposite is also true—belief and prayer are sure to result in spiritual power. So there is the challenge—get working and become a spiritual powerhouse for God.

ACTION response.

Think of just two ways you could improve your prayer life. Hey! Have you ever thought of getting a friend and praying together regularly. That's one idea.

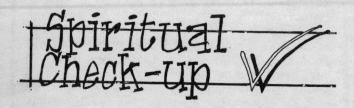

Spiritual Check-up ✓

Okay, what have you learnt about your heavenly Father from this chapter? Take your pen and list below just three characteristics of God you have discovered, e.g. He is more than ready to forgive us.

1. . . . .

2. . . . .

3. . . . .

Wise Words

'We readily admit that Jesus and all the genuine saints throughout history had spiritual power *and* that they had a deep prayer life. We believe that there must be some connection between their power and their life of prayer.'

Sherwood Eddy

'Seven days without prayer makes one weak.'

Allen Bartlett

'Prayer opens our eyes that we may see ourselves and others as God sees us.'

Clara Palmer

'Prayer is dangerous business. Results do come.'

G. C. Swain

'Prayer is not overcoming God's reluctance; it is laying hold of His highest willingness.'

a prayer

'Lord, I find praying so difficult;
Either I can't be bothered or there are
too many distractions around. Then at times
I'm just lazy. Lord, I know prayer is
important, help me to pray—please!'

7 Dropping out of church

What's your church like?

Is it:
- a) Really rather boring
- b) A good place to meet friends
- c) Okay
- d) Pretty dynamic
- e) A place I can get help
- f) Somewhere I can give something to
- g) A place I could take or leave
- h) Important to me
- i) Worthwhile

Some of you may think your church is great; but some of you may have had enough and be tempted to drop out. Maybe your church has got problems and you are critical of it. One Christian identified the real problem with the church when he said, 'The chief problem with the church is that you and I are in it'!

Think for a moment

I have a friend called John; I haven't seen him for

ages but he's still a friend. Anyhow, John is a really wonderful guy, a very practical person, very helpful, always eager to do things and extremely friendly. A few years ago he decided that he'd had enough and it was time to drop out of his home. I don't mean he jumped out of an upstairs window, but decided it was time to give up all that home represented. When people say they are dropping out or moving on, they usually mean that they are going to something 'that seems easier, or more fun, or both'. People drop out of school, out of jobs, out of a lot of things—and John wanted to drop out of where he'd lived. John felt that the fun of living there had gone away. He had his eye on a brand new place that would clear all those headaches. John could only see the defects, everything that was wrong with his old home, and a new environment and a new home was going to solve all his problems.

It's like that when we want a change of any sort. A weird sort of filter just slips over our eyes and all we seem to see are the bad points (whether real or imagined) of where we are, and the good points of where we think we would rather be.

It's the same with church. When people think of dropping out of the church, they see only its defects. 'If being a Christian is meant to be joyful why is church such a drag and so boring?' The sermons are dull and I can't understand them. The list goes on and on. Suddenly it seems almost easy to conclude that if God is perfect He couldn't possibly be behind all this.

There are a lot of reasons why people drop out of church, but no doubt they could all be listed under one heading: 'The Church Isn't Perfect'. That's right, the church isn't. Jesus promised to be with His church until the end of time. He did not promise to zap all its members or even all its leaders and

suddenly make them one hundred per cent wise and wonderful and thoroughly cool.

In all fairness we ought to have at least as much sympathy and understanding for the church as we do for anyone else. If your teacher gives one boring lecture, even though the others were brilliant, it's not quite fair to call the whole course rubbish and stomp off.

The church is made up of a 'pilgrim people' who are on a journey, struggling together. Some drop out, and when they do it might seem like a break for freedom and independence and a more carefree life. What they do not see until much later, sometimes never, is that when they break their journey they step off pretty much in the middle of nowhere.

The church isn't perfect (yet) but then we—that's

47

you and me, a few million other people and the Holy Spirit—aren't finished working on it either. So, if you're thinking of throwing it all in and going solo, have another think.

St. Augustine once said,

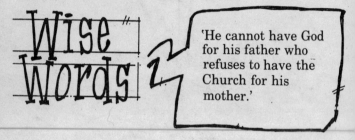

'He cannot have God for his father who refuses to have the Church for his mother.'

If you are a Christian, you are part of the Family of God. Don't wander off because you will get lost.

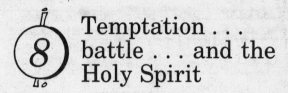

8 Temptation . . . battle . . . and the Holy Spirit

Thomas à Kempis wrote,

'There is no order so holy, no place so secret,
where there will be no temptation.'

Following Jesus Christ may lead to difficulty
because our loyalty to Him will certainly be tested.
The Christian life is not a bed of roses. It is a battle
ground; there is nothing to be afraid of, but it is
vital for you to realise that we are engaged in battle.
James tells us (1: 2) 'My brothers, consider your-
selves fortunate when all kinds of trials come your
way, for you know that when your faith succeeds in
facing such trials, the result is the ability to endure.'
Being tested by God and being tempted by the
Devil are different things and should not be
confused. In the New Testament the meaning of the
Greek word 'to tempt' means to test or to prove.
Peter writes in Chapter 1: 6 of his first letter,

'Be glad about this even though it may now be
necessary for you to be sad for a while because of

49

the many kinds of trials you suffer. Their purpose is to prove that your faith is genuine. Even gold, which can be destroyed is tested by fire, and so your faith which is much more precious than gold, must also be tested, so that it may endure. Then you will receive praise and glory and honour on the Day when Jesus Christ is revealed.'

While God *allows* the Devil to tempt us to do evil, He overrules the temptation as a test for our good. Paul tells Timothy to 'Endure hardship as a good soldier' (2 Timothy 2: 3). Paul can tell Timothy and tell us because he is a veteran himself in the battle against sin and temptation.

Temptation itself is not sin, of course. We know this because Jesus was tempted throughout His earthly life 'yet was without sin.' (Hebrews 4: 15) He was even led by the Holy Spirit into the desert to be tested by temptation. And He came out of it gloriously triumphant. But even then the Devil left Him only 'for a while' (Luke 4: 13).

The greatest saints (I love reading the lives of 'saints') have one thing in common: they all have been conscious of the Devil's activity. The more we seek to become holy, the more aware we shall become of the opposition. I can hear you saying, 'Well, why bother?' . . . Just read on!

Thoughts and desires which we know are wrong spring up from nowhere and they seem to flit around like birds wanting to build a nest in our minds, or to use Peter's illustration, they are like 'a roaring lion, looking for someone to devour' (1 Peter 5: 8).

Temptation becomes sin the moment the evil thought is invited into the mind, pondered and eventually acted upon (James 1: 13 – 15). The saying, 'You cannot prevent rooks flying over your head, but you can stop them building nests in your hat' applies well to this question of temptation. Therefore, as Christians, we have to be *alert*. We, like soldiers, must be determined to resist the first signs of attack. So a wrong thought should be thrown out *immediately*, a wrong attitude should be drowned before it comes tumbling out in words. We must also be sensible about all this. It's ridiculous if you are constantly bombarded with impure thoughts, to go to places, or mix with company where such thoughts are shared freely! Praying, 'Lead us not into temptation' and consciously putting yourself in the way of temptation won't help. We must be on our guard. We must occupy our minds with other things, and I personally believe we must be ready to avoid such places, no matter at what cost in terms of misunderstanding and loss of friendship. Anything is better than falling victim to the Devil.

Wise Words

'Be careful of your thoughts, they may break out into words at any moment.'

We must find our present weak points; those areas of our lives where we are specially vulnerable, so that we can protect them. Jesus said, 'Watch out and pray that you will not fall into temptation' (Mark 14: 38). That means watching so that you can avoid being caught unexpectedly. Watching also so that you can prevent yourself from running into any kind of danger. And praying because we cannot have the victory in our own strength; we need help from God.

1 Corinthians 10: 13 says 'No temptation has seized you except what is common to man. And God is faithful, he will not let you be tempted beyond what you can bear. But when you are tempted, He will also provide a way out so that you can stand up under it.'

Maybe this verse doesn't help you, and you feel that you've struggled hard but failed. You want to succeed but it doesn't seem to come. Or, as Paul once wrote looking back on a period of constant defeat in his own life, 'I do not understand what I do. For what I want to do I do not do, but what I hate, I do' (Romans 7: 15). What is the root cause of this common experience? Well, to start with, before we became Christians we had a tendency to sin because of our fallen nature. Although when we become Christians this tendency to sin (or self-centredness) does not leave us, it does not mean that we are bound towards a future full of defeat.

The only way to win is through God. Paul says in Romans 8: 2, 'through Christ Jesus the law of the Spirit of life set me free from the law of sin and death.' Here Paul, having cried out for help and deliverance from the grip of sin, is saying how God by the Holy Spirit has given it to him by bringing the life and power of the resurrected Jesus Christ into his heart. And so Paul continues in verse 37, 'in all these things we are more than conquerors through Him who loved us.'

The great missionary, Hudson Taylor, wrote:

'I prayed, fasted, agonised, strove, made resolutions, read the Bible more diligently, sought more time for retirement and meditation—but all without effect. Every day almost every hour, the consciousness of sin oppressed me. Then came the question, 'Is there no rescue? Must it be this to the end?—constant conflict, instead of victory, too often defeat?' I hated myself, I hated my sin, and yet I gained no strength in it.'

I have many times identified with his frustration. Hudson Taylor was desperate but he eventually found deliverance in *Christ*.

What was the secret of Christ's holy living? We don't have to search far in the Scriptures to find out. One day His disciples wanted Him to eat with them and He replied,

'my food is to do the will of Him that sent me and to finish His work'   (John 4: 34).

A little later He says to the unbelieving and critical Jews,

'I do always those things which please Him'
(John 8: 29).

No-one could deny it. He lived a life of complete obedience, and was the perfect example of holy living. All we need to do is to follow Him (phew! is that all?). But first, how are we to know what the will of God is? Secondly, when we have discovered it how are we going to do it?

God's answer is the Holy Spirit. First of all the Holy Spirit comes to dwell within us as soon as we become Christians.

'Whoever does not have the Spirit of Christ does not belong to Him.'   (Romans 8: 9)

It is the Holy Spirit's job to teach us all things

and to guide us into all truth (John 14: 26; 16: 13).
In other words He will reveal to us the Will of God
for us.

Secondly, He will enable us to obey that will, but
there are three important things we must be careful
not to do:

—'do not *resist* the Holy Spirit' (Acts 7: 51)
—'do not *quench* the Holy Spirit' (1 Thessalonians
5: 19)
—'do not *grieve* the Holy Spirit' (Ephesians 4: 30)

Instead of resisting the Holy Spirit, *surrender* to
Him; don't dictate what He can or cannot do; let
Him do as He wills. As for the word 'quench', it
means don't suppress the Holy Spirit, don't restrain
Him, or, as the dictionary puts it, don't 'withhold
Him from circulation.' Allow Him freedom to move
in your life. Allow Him to take control. Let God be
in charge.

Lastly, but not least, don't grieve Him. Don't
cause Him sorrow or distress by resisting and quen-
ching Him so that He cannot help you.

If we are sincerely willing to find God's will and
obey it, He will give us the power. Submitting our
wills to the will of God (surrendering) can be
described as 'the filling of the Holy Spirit.' It is an
act of God, in response to an attitude of willingness
on our part for God to have His way in our lives.

All Christians possess the Holy Spirit, but it is
quite another thing for Him to possess them. When
you and I received Christ we invited Him into the
whole of our lives, but perhaps we didn't allow His
Holy Spirit to possess us completely. That is why
some of us need a further encounter with Him. This
being 'possessed by the Holy Spirit', or 'being filled
by the Holy Spirit' is for many an experience which

is as tremendous as their conversion. But there are some who seek an emotional experience because someone else has had one. Now we all differ temperamentally and what may be a quiet, deliberate transaction with God for some, can involve an emotional upheaval for others. Both are to be found in the New Testament.

In my own life I am continually praying that the Holy Spirit may take more and more of my life and so fill me continually. The important thing is that we do not resist, quench or grieve. After that, we can leave the rest to Him. If He decides that A or B or C should happen, that's up to Him. This is what surrendering is all about. If Christ is to be Lord at all, He must be Lord of all. If not there will be defeat. If you want victory over sin you must get alone with the Master and willingly surrender all to Him. This is the first and fundamental step.

'Lord, Jesus, I take my hands off, as far as my life is concerned. I put you on the throne in my heart. Change, cleanse, use me as you choose. I take the full power of your Holy Spirit, I thank you.'
                              A prayer by William Borden.

The New Testament shows us that the Christian life is a life of faith. The problem with many of us is that we forget that faith is the link between our surrender to God and the consequences of that surrender.

So, what is faith, we ask? Blind faith means believing when there is no evidence to go on, but true faith is acting on God's promises. Given that we have met the conditions required, we believe that He will do what He said He would do. Having surrendered ourselves completely to Christ, we act in the belief that He will fill us with His Holy Spirit.

Now there is a part for us to play. Our spiritual life is not to be spent in an armchair.

In 1843 David Livingstone said, 'I am ready to go anywhere, provided it be forward.' Amen! Our faith must be fed and nourished if we are to win against sin. Our duty is to keep in vital touch with the source of our holiness. And if we are going to be holy we have to be in good form spiritually; Thomas Carlyle's comment here is very helpful,

'Holy in the German language "heilig" also means healthy; our English word 'whole', all of one piece without any hole in it, is the same word. You could not get any better definition of what holy is than healthy, completely healthy.'

Now the key to good spiritual health is daily training with the Lord.

One of the mistakes often made by Christians is to consider their feelings to be their spiritual thermometer. They are nothing of the kind! That is why so many Christians doubt even that they are Christians. They don't feel keen; they wonder what is wrong; then they begin to dig in the rubbish tip of *forgiven* sin and bring to light what our Father in Heaven has actually forgotten, and then they doubt whether He had ever cleaned them out at all. God says,

'and their sins and iniquities will I remember no more' (Hebrews 10: 17).

The practical way to victory in the Christian life is to spend time with God. It is then that faith is fed and holiness cultivated and victories won. Okay!!

These times with God are attacked more by the enemy than any other area of our Christian lives.

The last thing the Devil wants is for us to spend time with God. Yet nothing is more essential if we are to go forward in the spiritual life.

The closed door and stillness are what our Father requires in order to meet us,

'But when you pray, go to your room, close the door, and pray to your Father who is unseen. And your Father, who sees what you do in private will reward you.'

(Matthew 6: 6)

Of great importance during your time with God is your Bible reading. The purpose of Bible study is to discover more about our Master. Dig deep and you will be thrilled to discover the inexhaustible wealth of Christ.

The Devil, however, knows that those who are most able to resist him are those who study God's word and pray. Daniel tells us, 'the people who know their God will firmly resist him' (11: 32).

One excuse we give is that we have no time. But where there is a will there is a way. If we make time for so many other things in our lives, we can certainly make time to study God's Word.

We should try to study thoroughly with a determination to obey the truths which the Holy Spirit may reveal. It is easy to come to the Bible tired and anxious, just to scan a set passage, to close the Bible and to forget immediately what we've read. Spiritual growth does not come that way but through a teachable and listening heart. Go for it!

When you are tempted

Do you (a) try to push it out of your mind
        (b) play around with it
        (c) usually give in to it in the end
        (d) continually give in

The Bible gives some good advice:
'Resist the Devil and he will run away from you.'
                                    (James 4: 7)

When you are with a group of Christian friends
you might like to discuss these questions:

1. What are the most difficult temptations to
   resist?

2. When are the times when you are most
   successful in beating temptation?

3. Who is God the Holy Spirit?

4. What effect does the Holy Spirit have?

Wise Words

'The word "Comforter" as applied to the Holy
Spirit needs to be translated by some vigorous
term. Literally, it means "with strength". Jesus
promised His followers that "The Strengthener"
would be with them forever. This promise is no
lullaby for the faint-hearted. It is a blood trans-
fusion for courageous living.'

E. Paul Hovey

Mark Twain had the right idea when he said,
'There are several good protections against temptation, but the surest is cowardice.'

P.S. Just a few more words about the Holy Spirit

I feel that I missed out a few things in the last chapter, so here's an epilogue.

Often we think of the Holy Spirit as something injected into us—'Receive the Holy Spirit.' It is important to realise that the Holy Spirit is not a supernatural seed but God Himself who comes again and again in His creative power into our lives. 'Receive the Holy Spirit' actually means receive God. Receive the Spirit of God. The stress on *receiving* is because He is always *giving*. Now as He works in our lives He wants to give us more of His Holy Spirit. The Holy Spirit being the Spirit of Creation brings about growth.

So the reality of Him in us can be tested by the gradual growth of fruit. Fruit takes time to grow and often is hardly observed until ripe.

The fruit of the Spirit Paul says (in Galatians 5: 22ff) 'is Love, Joy, Peace, Patience, Kindness, Goodness, Faithfulness, Humility and Self-control.'

So what do you think? Do you have them? Are you going to produce them?

A good gardener always has an idea of what he

is trying to grow. Without vision even a cabbage patch will perish.

Now these fruits are not what you get at a village produce show (a prize marrow!). The fruits of the Spirit are those ways of thinking, speaking and acting which are brought about gradually by the Holy Spirit, as we allow Him, and spend time with Him. You cannot produce fruit without the root.

I don't think the Apostle Paul arranged his list of the fruits of the Spirit in just any order. I think they are progressive. First, *Love*. The living eternal seed from which all others come. Love is the budding point from which all the rest of the fruits of the Spirit grow. So to be unloving is to be out of touch with God. And God loves, not tolerates other people, but loves them. So the first sign that we are on His side and He on ours must be *at least* a tiny bud of His love breaking through our lives *to others*, starting with the people you live with.

Spiritual growth survey

Out of your group of friends or members of your family who may be Christian who would you say is the most—

    Joyful . . . .
    Patient . . . .
    Sensitive . . . .
    Trustworthy . . . .
    Kind . . . .
    Generous . . . .
    Loving . . . .
    Honest . . . .

Love, marriage and sex

Man has written more words about love than any other subject. Psychologists, philosophers, the world of literature and the arts all express it in different ways.

Interest in the subject of love has always been totally world-embracing. Certainly throughout recorded history, the searching for its real meaning has been continuous.

Love is possible at many levels, but today it is in danger of its worth being devalued, of selling it at a discount. It is also a tragedy that people have begun to assess love in terms of mere sexual performance.

Marriage is in deep trouble. Marriages are breaking up all around us. To many people marriage is regarded as square and old-fashioned. At the moment it would seem that the majority in our society believe in life-long monogamous marriage, but many, as the actual behaviour of our society reveals, do not.

Sex is special and valuable. If you owned a really valuable bracelet you are not going to wear it when you are gardening. If you receive a letter from someone very special you are not going to keep it with your bills. It is put in a special place. With this idea and thought of specialness as a measurement, it is surprising how many people today don't actually consider their sexuality as something unique and special. There are many how-to-do-it books. There is an abundance—instructing you how to enjoy sex while single, how to seduce others, how to have extra-marital affairs without your spouse finding out. T-shirts advertise 'do it' and now crude stickers on cars have become popular. The picture coming across through the media is that everybody does it, and so this kind of garbage has put a lot of pressure on Christians to conform.

Love

Almost everyone has experienced what he or she thought was love, only to find that it really wasn't; it was just emotion. It probably first happened early in the teen years (or is happening now!) when you were first attracted to a member of the opposite sex.

There was this strange, tingling excited feeling

that just would not go away. You probably felt you were walking on air, and then later you realised that was not love at all, it was just what you felt at the time. You were probably told it was 'puppy love', just infatuation. Unfortunately many people make mistakes because of not knowing how to handle adolescent emotions. It often leads to pre-marital sexual experience, which in turn often leads to pre-marital pregnancy. Tragically millions of babies are born or destroyed out of wedlock every year. Others leap into premature marriages, and stay married for the sake of the children or financial reasons, and are not in love at all! How sad.

The 'if' and 'because' love

Some people say 'I will love you if . . .' That's to say that it attaches requirements to your love.

'I will love you *if* you promise to marry me.'
'I will love you *if* you satisfy my desires.'
'I will love you *if* you go to bed with me.'

And unfortunately many people do not know any other kind of love. Another kind of love which often results in marriage is—'The love because of . . .' The basis is this: 'I love you because . . .' and then it is produced by a certain condition or quality in your life.

'I love you because you are pretty.'
'I love you because you give me security.'

It sounds pretty good because I want to be loved because of something in my life. What's wrong with that? Yes, all of us want to be loved because of something in our lives, and there really isn't anything wrong with that, but if that is the foundation and the source of your love then there is a problem. For example, if you are being loved because of certain qualities in your life, certain potential danger areas could become a reality. If the source of love is based on a certain quality or condition in your life—potential problems are envy, jealousy and competition. What happens when someone else comes along who has more of the qualities that you possess? This often happens when a beautiful secretary comes on the scene! It can easily make the other secretaries jealous.

Bible love

In the English language there is one word for love ... LOVE. In the Bible there are several different words in Greek translated as love in the English.

One of the words is *philia* from which the name of the City of Philadelphia comes, which means 'brotherly love'. Philia is friendship, companionship, the emotional sharing of time and interests. It shows a desire to co-operate.

Another word is *agape*. Agape is total Giving love. This is the love God expressed when he gave His only-begotten Son. He had no self-interest. He gave us His Son simply because He loved us. It is a love which involves thoughtfulness, concern and sensitivity to the needs of others.

Relevant to agape love in marriage, the Apostle Paul in Ephesians 5: 28 – 29 said, 'In this same way husbands ought to love (agape) their wives as their own bodies. He who loves his wife loves himself. After all, no one ever hated his own body, but he feeds and cares for it, just as Christ does the Church.'

You spell this love . . . GIVE! In a giving relationship there is no room for fear, frustration, pressure, envy or jealousy. Another Greek word for love is *Eros*. It is the root of the word erotic. H. Norman Wright in his book *Pillars of Marriages* defines eros as 'Love that seeks sensual expression.' It is a romantic desire inspired by the biology within us. Of itself eros is not wrong. But it should not act independently. Unfortunately it is the only love many people ever experience. But romantic, sensual love is only part of the God-given concept of total love.

The difference between eros and philia is that eros is a face-to-face relationship while philia is a shoulder to shoulder relationship. When applied to marriage it depicts a husband and wife working together. A friend is someone you want to be with. So, good marriages have philia love—in other words, husbands and wives who want to be with each other so

Philia makes your mate your friend

Agape goes far deeper. A love of total commitment, it means selflessness.

and

Eros produces romance—makes your mate become your lover.

Don't ever consider marriage unless it is built on a relationship of growing love. Don't marry for convenience, desire, security, money or any other reason. Marry because you have grown to love the person with whom you want to share the remainder of this life together.

66

Marriage is a sacrament like baptism and communion. The marriage service is not just a little extra religious seasoning to add flavour to married life. Marriage is an event at which God touches our lives in a powerful way to help us become all that we are meant to be. Marriage is more than making us feel all right about sex and what the neighbours might say. If it is right for two people to marry then God is present in everything related to it. Yes, that includes sex, not only sex, but all the other everyday things of cooking, gardening and decorating, the talking and the listening. God can be at the centre of our marriages if we allow Him that place, and if God is a strong fortress, and if He is at the centre of our marriage, then our marriage can be a strong fortress. My wife and I pray every morning together and talk about the Lord and talk to the Lord and we do the same just before we go to sleep. And if I am away we pray on the telephone. He is part of our thinking and decision making.

Is marriage to be permanent? Yes! Why? Simply because Jesus taught exactly that. Read Mark 10: 2 – 9 and Matthew 19: 3 – 9. Yes, this sounds like tough teaching and some people wished Jesus hadn't been so clear about it. Jesus, I believe, was clear about it because He was trying to safeguard marriages. Marriage is permanent. It is for life.

Sex ... when?

Why wait? So many people ask me that question. Only the other day a student asked me, 'Why do I have to wait? Is sex bad?' The reason you wait till marriage is because sex is so good. Because sex is so good it needs its proper setting. There are some ridiculous ideas that have been circulating around for years. One of them being that faithful married couples have sex just out of routine and that only the so-called swingers really tap the full potential of sex. Listen here, that is stupid! If God knows what is best for us (and He does), and His laws are intended to guide us toward real happiness, then the results will show that, won't they? And they do. (I don't know anyone, and I've talked to quite a few people, who waited for sex until their marriage and then felt they had been silly and cheated from all the excitement they could have had while the opportunities were going.) Sex is part of the eros love God designed. Sex when practiced in love and in the confines of marriage is holy and pure. The Apostle Paul said (Hebrews 13: 4), 'Marriage should be honoured by all, and the marriage bed (sex in marriage) kept pure, for God will judge the adulterer and all the sexually immoral.'

The word virginity has almost fallen out of use. Peer pressure and false or inbridled emotions have led to a great deal of pre-marital sex experimentation. The modern argument is, 'Those who have experienced intimate sexual relationships before marriage will be better sex partners in marriage.' However with the rising divorce rate the evidence suggests that this idea is wrong. The Bible also says this argument is wrong. God created us male and female and sex was designed only to be in the confines of marriage. Pre-marital sex is called fornication, and extra-marital sex is called adultery—both are capital offences against the Holy Law of God. Both adultery and fornication are wrong.

But sex practised in marriage, practised in love, is clean, holy and pure. The most obvious reason for sex is the reproduction of mankind, but there is another purpose. Sex can be the embodiment of all three of the Greek words of love: philia, agape and eros.

Sex has been designed by God to be the guiding force in preserving and perpetuating love between a husband and a wife.

One of life's greatest accomplishments is getting love, marriage and sex in the right order with the right person at the right time. Talk to God about your own thinking, feelings and desires and trust Him.

◁ ◁ ◁ ◁ ◁ ◁ ◁ ◁

Pornography

You are no doubt surprised that this heading appears in a book on the Christian life, but I couldn't believe my ears this summer when I was in Montreal, Canada. I met a Christian who felt it was all right to read pornographic magazines (he assured me that he didn't buy them ... his non-Christian brother had bought them). He also assured me that it was having no effect on him. He was either a liar or not human!

If you find pornographic pictures interesting then this chapter is for you. However, you can still read the chapter if you don't find them interesting!

There is nothing evil about beauty, but if you find that your eye catches a picture of a woman in the nude and you still want to look at it—what does that say about you? And what are the consequences? Probably what is happening is like seeing an incredibly fantastic red sports car driving down the wrong way on a one way street—what your eyes have seen is really quite beautiful but what might happen is not!

O.K., where do we start? Well, firstly, it's worth saying that our bodies are indeed very, very beautiful. Ever since the cavemen, artists and sculptors have endeavoured to communicate this fact.

But this beauty does carry some possible danger with it.

Our appreciation of beauty leads to a sense of attraction. We like what we see. So, what is wrong with a healthy appreciation of what may be a beautiful naked body? Why is looking at a pornographic magazine wrong? It is wrong because it is a perversion of what God has given to us. It directs our good natural appreciation in the wrong direction. It treats sex as something that can be practised with anyone you like and the person in the picture becomes an object of our lust and unnatural sexual fantasies.

Pornography like so many other evils is a situation where beauty has been corrupted. To quote Shakespeare, 'Lilies that fester smell far worse than weeds.' So, so true. What Shakespeare is saying (I think), if something is beautiful, then the more awful and messed up it becomes if it is abused.

What would Jesus say about pornography? Well He did say this: 'Anyone who looks lustfully at a woman has already committed adultery with her in his heart.' No, you couldn't really get anything clearer could you? There is a law against rape, but there isn't a law against you looking at pornographic pictures. But Jesus links the two, for thought and action are very close together. Magazines like Playboy dehumanise the woman, and when men dehumanise women, they dehumanise themselves. The woman is just a disposable item. Looking at a pornographic picture (by choice) is actually taking something we have no right to take.

Pornography sows seeds that can fester into more wrong. There are many cases heard in courts where the defendant admits that the urge to commit a crime came directly from viewing pornographic material.

Beware. If you have copies I suggest you get rid of them. Maybe speaking to someone like a minister would help, so you can be prayed for and set free from the habit. If your eyes catch pornographic pictures don't keep them fixed there—move them away. As you consciously decide and pray for God's strength you will discover the peace of God in your life.

Scripture Spotlight

'For this reason a man shall leave his father and mother and be joined to his wife, and the two shall become one flesh. So they are no longer two but one flesh. What therefore God has joined together, let not man put asunder.'

(Matthew 19: 5, 6)

Talk it over

1. What do you think makes a good marriage?
2. What should be distinctive about a Christian marriage?
3. What sort of things should you consider before getting married?

4. Should wives always obey their husbands (see Ephesians 5: 22)?
5. Under what circumstances did Jesus say divorce was permissible?
6. Is being single a second best situation, or does it have its good aspects?
   'Marriage can be a foretaste of heaven or an anticipation of hell.'

Wise Words

'Marriages may be made in heaven, but man is responsible for the maintenance work.'
                                              Anon.
'God, the best maker of all marriages, Combine your hearts in one.'
                                William Shakespeare
                                Henry V, Act V, Sc.2

11 Tongue talk

Before you begin this chapter I would like you to think about the questions below. Be honest with yourself.

When did you last

    (a)   say something untrue about someone else?
    (b)   say something unkind?
    (c)   run someone down by what you said about them?
    (d)   verbally lash out at someone?
    (e)   regret something you said?
    (f)   help to spread gossip?
    (g)   use God's name as a swear word?

If you said 'never' to all of the above questions you are a saint. Now read on:

Aesop, the philosopher of the Fables, was asked one day what was the most useful thing in the world. 'The tongue', he replied. And what (they asked), is the most harmful thing in the world? 'The tongue', he replied once more.

I think Aesop was right when he said that the tongue is the most harmful thing in the world. It is the only tool that grows sharper with constant use! The Apostle James writing two thousand years ago said that the tongue, though only a small part of the body, can do enormous damage. And for two thousand years, millions of tongues have proven the truth of that statement (many of us Christians are part of that number!).

I want to devote this chapter to the use of the tongue because I know in my own life that my tongue has got me into some awkward situations, and I believe that the tongue causes us more problems than anything else, and it is rarely ever taught or preached about in Church. You only need a spark to start a forest fire and as we look at the history of the Church, it is obvious that there has been much damage done just through the sparks of the tongue. I have spoken to many people broken by the words of others. No doubt I have wounded others with words, and haven't even known it. I hear myself say things I wish I hadn't, and hear things said that I wish I'd never heard.

Words are often tragically destructive and unless we seek God's way, our words will continue to hurt rather than heal. I was speaking to someone recently who had been crushed and battered by words, and my response was 'Oh, don't worry, they are only words.' How untrue this popular saying is.

'Sticks and stones may break my bones, but words will never harm me.' What a useless thing to say to someone. Just words! It's like saying, 'After all, it's just an atom bomb!'

How do we deal with the tongue when we are constantly exposed to negative degrading speech on a daily basis? From words chosen by a colleague or boss at work to the crude language on television; to casual conversations with neighbours, to careless chatter among Christian friends—we are exposed constantly to corrupted communication (no wonder our minds need renewing!) and if all this junk is going into us . . . where does it go?

Our words can destroy our relationship with God, our relationship with those we love the most, and even our relationship with ourselves. Having a tongue is like having dynamite in our dentures.

Looking at the subject in the Bible amazed me. There was so much about it. I doubt there is any single subject that occupies more space in Scripture than the use of our tongue and our mouth.

God gave us the power to speak. He gave us His own authority and creative ability. The Bible tells us that it was by God's words that all creation was brought into being.

'The Lord created the heavens by His command, the sun, moon and stars by His spoken word.'
Psalm 33: 6

and

'It is by faith that we understand that the Universe was created by God's word.' Hebrews 11: 3

It is only reasonable that we give considerable

thought to the way we use the power.

Jesus talks about the tongue and relates it to a tree and its fruit.

'To have good fruit you must have a healthy tree; if you have a poor tree, you will have bad fruit. A tree is known by the kind of fruit it bears. You snakes—how can you say good things when you are evil? For the mouth speaks what the heart is full of.' Matthew 12: 33

The heart is the tree and the mouth is the fruit of the tree. The tree is known by its fruit. Therefore what comes out of your mouth is the indication of what is in your heart. Jesus then goes on to apply this very specifically to our words

'The good man brings good things out of the good stored up in him, and the evil man brings evil things out of the evil stored up in him.' Matthew 12: 35

It seems as though He is saying there's no middle-road between good or evil. It's either good all the way or evil all the way. It's the same stream all the way through.

Before we look at how we can deal with the problem let us outline the individual difficulties that are involved in the use of the tongue and what we say.

1.Gossip

Gossip, slander and rumours can destroy people! We all know we shouldn't gossip. Yet our thirst for the 'news', both hearing and telling it, seems at times insatiable, so we devise ways of sharing it. Can I share something for prayer! That excuse soothes our consciences. The only time people dislike gossip is when the gossip is about them. And if my friend gossips to me about someone else, should I not doubt my friend's loyalty? After all, if he gossips to me, maybe he will gossip *about* me.

A mother wrote to a woman's magazine column asking the counsellor what to do about the rumour being spread that her 16–year old daughter was pregnant. The mother wondered if the best thing to do would be to transfer her daughter to another school. The counsellor suggested not; instead let time prove the rumour false. It sounded like good sensible advice. The mother however wrote back months later saying that she did leave her daughter in the same school and now they are saying that she had an abortion. What should she do now? The counsellor had no reply. Once rumours begin it really is tough to win.

The most devastating thing about rumours, whether true or false, is that they are irretrievable. There is a story of a man who went to see a monk during the Middle Ages. He told the monk that he had sinned because he had been gossiping and telling slanderous things about someone. What should he do? The monk told him to go and put a feather on every doorstep in the town. The man quickly rushed away and did just that. He then came back to the monk. The monk told him to go back and pick up all the feathers. The man said that would be impossible as by now the wind would have blown them all away. The monk told the man that is what had happened with his words. Quite challenging don't you think? Don't despair . . . hang on till the end of the chapter.

I've put gossip and slander together because as someone once said they are like cousins. While gossip is often spoken in the context of idle careless chatter, slander is the open intentional sharing of damaging information.

There are many references in the Bible to gossip and slander. Here are a few.

'You shall not go up and down as a slanderer among your people.' Leviticus 19: 16

'The words of a whisperer are like delicious morsels, they go down into the inner parts of the body.' Proverbs 18: 8

'Gossip is so tasty—how we love to swallow it.' Proverbs 18: 8 (Good News)

Do you know that it is possible to destroy somebody with words?
Jeremiah's enemies said

'Come, and let us smite him with the tongue and let us not give heed to any of his words.' Jeremiah 18: 8

and in the New Testament we read:

'They get into the bait of being idle and going about from house to house. And not only do they become idlers, but also gossips and busy-bodies, saying things they out not to.' 1 Timothy 5: 13

'If any of you suffers, it must not be because he is a murderer or a thief or a criminal or meddles in other people's affairs.' 1 Peter 4: 15

Isn't it remarkable that the busy-body is listed in company with murderers and criminals. Most Christians would be horrified to be classified as murderers and criminals, but many are busy-bodies.

Gossip and slander are obviously serious violations of God's will. Why then are they so widespread? Probably because we have neutralised ourselves with what we call 'good' excuses. They are not good excuses, but myths, and recognising them will help us to remove them from our conversation.

Myth Number One
The people when told won't tell anyone else. They promised they wouldn't and we were sharing in confidence. Is this true?

Myth Number Two
I am just sharing this so we can pray about it. It normally comes out as 'Let me tell you this so that you can pray more intelligently.' It this true? Is prayer our real motive?

Myth Number Three
If the information is true then it is fine to share it. Nothing could be further from the truth. The issue is not whether the information is true or false, but whether it is harmful or confidential.

'Do not use harmful words, but only helpful words, the kind that build up and provide what is needed, so that what you say will do good to those who hear you.'   Ephesians 4: 29

2. Lying
Augustine said, 'When regard for truth has been

broken down or even slightly weakened, all things will remain doubtful.'

A lying tongue is included in the infamous list in Proverbs 6

'There are seven things that the Lord hates and cannot tolerate,

A proud look
A lying tongue
Hands that kill innocent people
A mind that thinks up wicked plans
Feet that hurry off to do evil
A witness who tells one lie after another
And a man who stirs up trouble among friends.'
Proverbs 6: 16–19

Out of those seven sins that are hated by God three relate to the tongue: a lying tongue, a false witness and stirring up trouble or, as the RSV translates it, 'sowing discord'. Proverbs 12: 22 confirms this:

'Lying lips are an abomination to the Lord.'

The word 'abomination' is the strongest word that can be used to describe something that displeases God. On the other hand, the rest of that verse tells us,

'but those who act faithfully are His delight.'

The reason truth is so important to God is because truthfulness is part of His nature. Psalm 31: 5 tells us that He is a 'God of truth' and in Titus 1: 2 we read of God 'who does not lie.' So our desire and commitment for truth draws us nearer to God and into deeper fellowship with Him. God's word commands us to speak the truth regardless of the cost. Therefore our hearts and consciences cannot be clear before God and our joy cannot be full if we get involved with that which is false.

Oliver Wendell Holmes said,

'Sin has many tools, but a lie is the handle that fits them all.'

Lying against the truth is the strength of Satan's system. Not only does he lie, but he wants us to lie as well. And when we lie we support him. That's exactly what Jesus was saying when He said to the Pharisees

'You are the children of your father, the Devil, and you want to follow your father's desires. From the very beginning he was a murderer and has never been on the side of truth, because there is no truth in him. When he lies, he speaks his native language, for he is a lier and the father of lies.'
John 8: 44

Non-truth is the Devil's language and the language of the world. So we must be wise and beware. Non-truth is the sin that Satan promotes, whether it be lying to cover up adultery or deceiving to gain some business advantage or bearing false witness. Non-truth supports, promotes and protects the welfare of SIN. It is the supporting structure of Satan's system.

3. Negative talk

This is one of the "respectable sins" practised by Christians. Usually it isn't considered a SIN.

'This is never going to work out.'

'I know things are going to go wrong.'

The words may all be very polite and respectable but in many cases they are unacceptable to God.

'Thoughtless words can wound as deeply as any sword, but wisely spoken words can heal.' Proverbs 12:18

Many of us dig our own graves with mouths. In Numbers 13 we have an account of the spies who were sent into the promised land. All twelve spies saw the same thing and all had the same experience. Ten of them came back and said, 'Oh, it's a good land, but it's full of giants. The cities are walled up to heaven and we were like grasshopers in our own sight.'

Two spies said, 'It's a wonderful land. Let's go in and take it.' The contrast is evident (Numbers 13: 30). Joshua and Caleb said, 'We are able,' the other ten said, 'we are not able.' Every one of them sealed his destiny by what he said and what he thought. Christians do that time and time again. The ten spies who were negative ignored God's potential, and were quick to jump to the wrong conclusion. The grumbling Israelites said, 'Why is the Lord taking us into that Land? We will be killed in battle, and our wives and children will be captured. Wouldn't it be better to go back to Egypt.'

Once the grumbling started, the wrong conclusions were easy to sell. Not only that, but it led to self-pity (14: 2): 'It would have been better to die in Egypt or even here in the wilderness.'

Negative talkers often feel very sorry for themselves. And it leads to an atmosphere of fear, rebellion and dissatisfaction. 'Majority reports' are not always true.

Anyhow God's judgement on the Israelites was swift and final. They would not see the Promised Land!

But is it ever right to express dissatisfaction? Yes of course—so long as it is constructive and helpful, for our trust should be in God and what He is able to achieve and do through and for us in each situation. Fix your eyes upon JESUS, and the good that He can bring out of each circumstance.

4. Flattery and boasting
I don't think most people understand how dangerous flattery is, and how unacceptable it can be to God. As a preacher I appreciate genuine gratitude from people, but I'm learning to be on my guard because many preachers have been ensnared by flattery. There is a great deal of insincerity among Christians—a lot of sweet talk that really doesn't amount to anything.

Parties often thrive on bigger and better boasts. The boaster is the person who keeps the conversation circulating around himself and his accomplishments. It seems alright because you're not harming anyone, and if you've got something to say, then say it. Some people think that if they don't praise themselves, then no-one else will! These are excuses that are very shallow. Even the basic rules of communication dictate that we talk about the interests of others and not only of ourselves. I was really challenged about this several years ago when I met someone who talked non-stop about themselves. After half an hour, feeling quite bored, the thought occurred—am I like that when I talk to others? That day I made a decision, that outside of close friends and family I would ask about others rather than talk about my self (I hope I've improved).

> 'Don't do anything from selfish ambition or from a cheap desire to boast, but be humble towards one another, always considering others better than yourselves.' Philippians 2: 3

The Greek words for "from a cheap desire to boast" mean empty and glory—so this is the glorification of emptiness—the promotion of our nothingness.
And as for flattery, Psalm 12: 1 – 3 says

> 'Help us, Lord!
> There is not a good man left;
> honest men can no longer be found.
> All of them lie to one another,
> they deceive each other with flattery.
> Silence those flattering tongues O Lord.'

As I said earlier, that does not mean we should never genuinely compliment, encourage or praise someone who is deserving of it. But we should ask the question, 'Why am I complimenting this person?' If it is to encourage and support them then it is a compliment and not flattery. Compliments that give God the glory, shield others from the traps of pride. Often, however, the problem is that those receiving it don't know how to react. The secret is to react with humility. Humility is to receive praise and to pass it on to God untouched by you. True—but how hard that is. It takes many years of God working in us to do that. A good example of course is Mother Teresa of Calcutta, who is genuinely a very humble person despite all the good she does.

Let us be careful about boasting and flattery and pray along with the Psalmist,

'May the words of my mouth and the meditation of my heart be pleasing in Your sight O Lord, my Rock and my Redeemer.'   Psalm 19: 14

5. *Excessive talking*
Connected to number four is excessive talking.

'The more you talk, the more likely you are to sin.
If you are wise, you will keep quiet.'
                    Proverbs 10:19

'The more you worry, the more likely you are to have bad dreams, and the more you talk, the more likely you are to say something foolish.' Ecclesiastes 5: 3

If a person talks all the time, he is simply telling you what he is—for 'a fool's voice is known by the multitude of his words'.

Furthermore, bear in mind that Jesus said, 'out of the abundance of the heart, the mouth speaks.' A restless tongue indicates a restless heart. A person who can never keep quiet is not at rest, no matter how much he may talk about peace and joy. Speaking without thinking is shooting without aiming!

ACTION response.

Think before you open your mouth—it helps.

6. Hastiness with your words

'Do you see a man who is hasty in his words? There is more hope for a fool than for him.' Proverbs 29: 20

That's a very searching statement. Don't immediately say everything you feel the moment you feel it. To do so is very dangerous.

In Psalm 106 we have a rather tragic picture of Moses who lost the privilege of leading God's people into the promised land because of one rash sentence that he spoke. The Children of Israel were complaining about not having water and God told Moses,

'Go ahead with the people and speak to the rock. When you speak to it the water will come out.'

Moses had previously brought water out of a rock by hitting it with his rod, but because he was really angry with the people, instead of doing what God said, he impatiently hit the rock and said,

'Must we bring forth water for you rebels?'

God honoured him and the water came out, but afterwards in a private discussion with Moses, God said,

'Moses, you've lost the privilege of leading my people into the promised land because you didn't honour me with your words.'

God warns us against hastiness, so be careful of what you say.

7. *Immoral speech*
Immoral expressions are not compatible with our new life in Jesus Christ. I am amazed at how often people (including ministers!) enjoy telling 'dirty jokes'. These jokes, stories, and words are rejected by the Bible.

'Since you are God's people, it is not right that any matters of sexual immorality or indecency or greed should even be mentioned among you. Nor is it fitting for you to use language which is obscene, profane or vulgar . . .' Ephesians 5: 3 – 12

It seems that television has been the most influential instrument in numbing Christian attitudes about decency and purity. Films laced with obscene language and with sexual experiences graphically protrayed are harmful, yet so many Christians seem prepared to sit and watch it and take it in. No wonder some Christians enjoy listening to dirty jokes because their minds are filled with dirty things. Perhaps we have deceived ourselves into thinking that we can be observers without it affecting our talk and our lifestyle. We are becoming dangerously open to the input of immorality and ungodliness. Tragically, this input soon shows up in our output.

As they say in computer programming,

'Garbage in, garbage out.'

Obviously all this kind of speech is damaging; instead of building up it tears down. It weakens our resistance to immorality and it does not benefit those who listen.

In Ephesians 5 we read that we should stand before God as a holy person. We have been made righteous in Christ (right with God when we became Christians). Our goal as growing believers is to match our standing before God with our living. Therefore crude talk has no place in the Christian's life.

8. *Using God's name in vain.*

> 'You shall not misuse the name of the Lord your God, for the Lord will not hold anyone guiltless who misuses His Name.' Exodus 20: 7

Quite clear isn't it! He not only includes this one in the Ten Commandments, but the ending of it is the sternest of them all.

Essentially to take God's name in vain means to use it as though it has no worth or value.

And I think it's true to say that a lot of people don't appreciate the real value of God's Name. God's Name has a real value and worth. The significance of God's name must be looked at in two ways. Its significance to God and its significance to us.

God's Name is a revelation of His Glory. His Name communicates His Being, His Character. The Psalmist said,

> 'I will declare your Name . . .' Psalm 22: 22

Expressing that his desire is to speak about all that God is.

In Exodus 3: 13 – 15 we read the story of Moses and the burning bush.

'When I go to the Israelites and say to them, "The God of your ancestors sent me to you," they will ask me, "What is His Name?" So what can I tell them?' God said, 'I AM who I AM. This is what you must say to them, "The One who is called I AM has sent me to you.'

God's name revealed who He was and is.

This is also true in the names of Our Lord Jesus Christ. His names reveal His character, worth and work. The name Jesus means Saviour. It is a very special and precious name.

The name of Jesus carries power over evil spirits (Matthew 7: 22) and power in prayer (John 14: 13 – 14). It is the authority by which the Holy Spirit comes (John 14: 26). It is the authority for salvation (Romans 10: 13) and baptism (Matthew 28: 19 – 20). Paul writes,

'For this reason God raised him to the highest place above and gave him the name that is greater than any other name, that at the name of Jesus every knee should bow, in heaven and on earth and under the earth, and every tongue confess that Jesus Christ is Lord, to the Glory of God the Father.'   Philippians 2: 9 – 11

Therefore when we use one of His names in an empty, negative context we are degrading Him. Not only is His name significant to Him but it should be so for us.

My wife's name is Killy—it is precious to me. Killy is the name of someone I love very much. If people used my wife's name casually and flippantly it would concern me—so it should concern us when God's name is used by people, especially Christians, in a callous way. Expressions such as 'Oh, God' and 'My Lord' are often used as verbal exclamation points; but sadly people use worse expressions than those. Even expressions like 'Praise the Lord' are thrown about with such frequency that they become empty religious phrases. In one place where I was staying, during breakfast one of the hosts said, 'Pass the toast over, praise the Lord.'—I couldn't believe what I was hearing—I just let it go. *And I should have said something.*

As we grow in the Lord, Jesus becomes much more precious to us and His Name becomes one that we love. And increasing awareness of all that God is makes us realise how special His Name is.

That's quite a long list—I've mentioned eight areas of concern. You've probably had enough and feel flaked out. Well, maybe you ought to take a break before reading the next bit!

Curing the problem

1. Recognise mis-use of the tongue as a problem of your heart and mind
We've already seen it in Matthew 12: 33 – 34 that the problem is in our hearts. James 3: 10 – 12 confirms this. Therefore we need to understand Proverbs 4: 23,

'Keep your heart with all diligence for out of it are the issues of Life.'

The mouth is the barometer of the heart.

2. Confess your sins, be cleansed and forgiven

Many people would not want to use the word 'sin' in describing their mis-use of the tongue. But when we come to grips with it as sin we'll begin to see some results. Repentance is required for the cleansing of sin. It is not just 'feeling sorry' but an acknowledgement that your relationship with God has been affected. So it is a wanting to say sorry with a view to changing and, by the strength of God and the power of the Holy Spirit, you can change.

'If we confess our sins to God He will keep His promise and do what is right; He will forgive us our sins and purify us from all our wrongdoing.'
1 John 1: 9

3. Refuse evil and yield to God
Paul says in Romans 6: 12 – 13, firstly that we are to *deny* the Devil access to the use of our bodies. Tell the Devil 'You can't have my hands, you can't have my feet and you can't have my tongue.' Secondly, *yield yourself to God.*

Deliberately tell God that you want your heart and your tongue to be an instrument of righteousness and that you are yielding them to Him for that purpose. Pray as the Psalmist did,

'Create in me a clean heart, O God, and renew a right spirit within me.' Psalm 51: 10

4. Understand why you have a tongue
The Scriptures tell us,

'Therefore my heart is glad and my tongue rejoices, my body also will rest secure.'
Psalm 16:9

Peter in Acts 2: 26 quotes this psalm,

'Your tongue should rejoice and give God the
Glory.'

5. Decide to praise God
Praise is the result of a decision. That is why David
said, 'My heart is fixed. I will give thanks.' At one
time David was in the court of the Philistine king
running away to save his life and yet—

'I will bless the Lord at all times;
His praise shall continually be in my mouth.
My soul shall make her boast in the Lord.
. . . Oh magnify the Lord with me, and let
us exalt His Name together.' Psalm 34: 1 – 3

6. Submit to the discipline of the body
One realm of our lives which is definitely subject to
the discipline of the body is the way we talk about
one another.

'If your brother sins against you, go and show him
his fault, just between the two of you.'
Matthew 18: 15 – 17

That's discipline. Don't go and tell everybody else
first. That's the normal reaction of many Christians.
If somebody upsets me, I don't tell him—I tell everybody except the brother who offended me. Then it
is even harder to heal the breach later.

Therefore, if somebody does something wrong,
first, go and speak directly to the person concerned
in order to avoid the breach. *Secondly* (and this is
where most people slip up), if somebody comes to

you and says, 'Do you know what Brother Jones or Sister Smith said about me?' remember to ask, 'Have you spoken to Brother Jones or Sister Smith?' If the reply is 'no', then say, 'Well, don't speak to me!' Now that is real discipline. Otherwise you can become an accessory after the fact. In legal terms you become responsible for blowing up the situation and making a breach in the body of Christ.

In conclusion (at long last!), if, after this chapter, you have realised that you have sinned with your tongue, or have any of the problems covered, I suggest you apply these remedies and confess your problem now as a sin. If you have hurt another Christian, you may need to go to him and ask him to forgive you.

Face the truth about your sin and ask God to forgive you. Ask Him to cleanse you; accept His forgiveness and pray to be filled with His Holy Spirit.

I have raised a lot of ideas that maybe you have not considered before. When you next get the opportunity with friends or Bible Study group, discuss what you think about the eight issues I have mentioned. Just to remind you, they are:

1. Gossip
2. Lying
3. Negative talk
4. Flattery and boasting

5. Excessive talking
6. Hastiness with your words
7. Immoral speech
8. Using God's name in vain.

Is there anything you would like to add to the list?

Wise Words

'It is no great thing to be humble when you are brought low; but to be humble when you are praised is a great and rare attainment.'

St. Bernard of Clairvaux

'The deeds we do, the words we say,
Into still air they seem to fleet,
We count them ever past;
But they shall last—
In the dread judgment they
And we shall meet.'

John Keble

Remember it . . . Remember what? . . . The Sabbath!

Someone once said that man is an able creature, but he has made 32,647,389 laws and hasn't yet improved on the Ten Commandments. In the Ten Commandments we have, in summary form, guidelines for Christian living. It is worth spending time meditating on them, and by the grace of God and His Holy Spirit, putting them into practice. A former Archbishop of Canterbury, William Temple, said,

'Love of God is the root, love of our neighbours the fruit, of the Tree of Life. Neither can exist without the other, but the one is cause and the other effect, and the order of the Two Great Commandments must not be inverted.'

In this chapter I would like to look at one of the Commandments, as it is one that is often in the news —the fourth Commandment.

'Remember the Sabbath day by keeping it holy. Six days you shall labour and do all your work

95

but the seventh day is a Sabbath to the Lord your God. On it you shall not do any work, neither you, nor your son or daughter, nor your manservant or maidservant, nor your animals, nor the alien within your gates. For in six days the Lord made the heavens and the earth, the sea, and all that is in them, but He rested on the Seventh day. Therefore, the Lord blessed the Sabbath and made it holy.'   Exodus 20: 8

People have more differences of opinion over this Commandment than any other. Therefore it can be confusing and difficult to discover what God is saying to us. Let us then be prepared for God to challenge us on everything in relation to the Sabbath, so that we may be able clearly to understand what God means.

Possibly the reason why God spells this Commandment out in greater detail than any other is because He realised we would try to get round it in some way, thinking up all kinds of excuses why we should not obey it.

I think it's right first of all to clear away what can always be a problem about this Commandment, mainly that the Sabbath day in the Old Testament is the seventh day which is our Saturday. But now, as Christians, we observe Sunday. Why? All we can say is that in God's providence He allowed the early Church to observe Sunday, the first day of the week, as the Sabbath, because the first day of the week is the day Jesus rose from the dead. It is the central day of the Christian calendar.

The fourth Commandment begins with 'Remember'—the Sabbath day was already being observed by the people of Israel before the Law was given on Sinai.

'Remember'—from the moment of Creation God

required you to observe a day of rest, which makes good sense. Therefore the Sabbath day is not an afterthought and is just as important as the other nine Commandments.

It is part and parcel of God's law—for sound living, and is not done away with in the New Testament any more than any of the other nine.

And yet it is true to say that we break this one more than the others—or we more obviously break it. We see that more and more things happen on Sunday than used to.

The evanglist, D. L. Moody, preaching a sermon in 1880 was lamenting the fact that people were no longer observing Sundays as they used to do.

'You want power in your Christian life do you?
You want Holy Ghost power?
You want the dew of heaven on your brow?
You want to see men convicted and converted?
I don't believe that we will ever have any
genuine conversions until we get straight
on this Law of God. Men seem to think that
they have a right to change a Holy day into
a holiday, and nowadays young Christians have
more temptations to break the Sabbath than
we had forty years ago in 1840.'

He was basically saying we must stop the rot if we are Christians. Reading Moody's sermon we realise that we are much further down the line than he was then. He was talking about trains and buses starting to run on a Sunday. But most of us have accepted trains and buses running on a Sunday since the day we were born—and the trouble with this Commandment is that each generation accepts more and more, and Sunday becomes less and less a day of rest and a day for the Lord.

Therefore what do we do as Christians?

Do we buy petrol on Sunday?

Do we buy newspapers?—If we do it makes other people work. What are the things we should and should not do?

The great danger is that we accept things in our materialistic world because we have always known them like that. However, this Commandment asks us to challenge our ways of going about things that were established as normal practice before we were born—and that is a very big challenge from God.

It is right for us to challenge the Abortion Laws because we believe that God's standard is at stake. But, what about the standards of Sunday when the practices for so long have been different from what the Bible teaches us?

Some of you may be thinking, 'Since we've entered into the freedom of the Spirit we don't want to get bogged down about keeping the Sabbath day holy'—which meant so much legalism in the Church in the past. In no sense are we wanting to bring back legalism but I believe that Moody is right when he said that every Command of God is there to be obeyed, and unless we obey them, then we will not have the spiritual power.

'Remember six days you shall work . . .' Sometimes we need to emphasise this part of the Commandment, and I'm not talking about those who are unemployed. Rest on the seventh is dependent on the six working days. For some people who have to work on Sunday like doctors, nurses, police . . . well the key here is to do six days' work and the *seventh* is a day of rest. So, if you have to work on Sunday, when is your seventh day—is that your Sabbath?

The Commandment tells us that the Sabbath is

1. a day of rest
2. a day dedicated to God

Let us look at how Jesus dealt with the Sabbath—

'One Sabbath Jesus was going through the corn-
fields, and as His disciples walked along, they
began to pick some ears of corn. The Pharisees
said to Him, "Look, why are they doing what is
unlawful on the Sabbath?" He answered, "Have
you never read what David did when he and his
companions were hungry and in need? In the days
of Abiathar the high priest, he entered the house
of God and ate the consecrated bread, which is
lawful only for priests to eat. And he also gave
some to his companions." Then He said to them,
"The Sabbath was made for man and not man for
the Sabbath. So the Son of Man is Lord even of
the Sabbath." '   Mark 2: 23 – 28

What had happened with the Sabbath Law at the
time of Jesus was that the Scribes and Pharisees
had taken what was a good Law of God and hemmed
it in with petty regulations—and that makes the
Sabbath a burden—so Jesus takes issue with this.
Jesus says it is not a burden. Sabbath was made for
man's good and in the Gospels this is explained.
This is God's Law but don't be stupid with it. Understand its true meaning.

In Matthew 12 Jesus allowed works of necessity
on the Sabbath. 'If an ox needs a drink then lead it
to water.' Secondly he allowed works of emergency.
'If an ass falls into a pit you don't say "I'll come
tomorrow." ' Just as if our chimney was on fire, we
don't say we will ring the Fire Brigade on Monday.
And, thirdly, he allowed works of mercy. What
should you do—'good or evil?' It is obvious we should

do works of mercy and goodness. It is obviously right to visit a sick person. Jesus says we must be sensible. But the great danger is when Jesus says you must be sensible—we say 'oh yes' and therefore include everything under that heading.

Good guide lines

Jesus allows works of necessity
Jesus allows works of emergency
Jesus allows works of mercy

—and these things are in fact exceptions to the general rule that we stop work on a Sabbath.

A good example is Eric Liddell (see the film 'Chariots of Fire'). He refused to compete in an Olympic race because it was to be held on a Sunday.

There is a law in the Old Testament that when the Children of Israel came into the promised land as a nation they were told, 'Give a Sabbath rest to the land every seven years.' One year in every seven don't work the land, and if you keep that law you will receive as much in six years as you would in seven.

For 490 years the people of Israel disobeyed that command and then they were taken into exile by Nebuchadnezzar. When they were in exile, out of the land of Israel, they were obviously receiving no produce from the land.

—For how many years?—70
Note 7 x 70 years = 490 years

They were told by God to give a Sabbath year every seven but they did not and God took it back from them.

I believe that is a picture that is very important—if we don't give the Sabbath to God He will take it—the blessing that God wants to give may not come.

Scripture Spotlight

'God blessed the seventh day and sanctified it; because in it He had rested from all His work which He created and made.'

Genesis 2: 3

'Remember the sabbath day, to keep it holy. Six days you shall labour, and do all your work; but the seventh day is a Sabbath to the Lord your God.'

Exodus 20: 8 – 10a

'This is the day which the Lord has made; let us rejoice and be glad in it.'

Psalm 118: 24

Wise Words

'If the Sabbath goes, everything else goes with it'
Marion Lawrence

'You show me a nation that has given up the Sabbath and I will show you a nation that has got the seeds of decay'

Dwight L. Moody

'I think the world of today would go mad, just frenzied with strain and pressure, but for the blessed institution of Sunday'
said in the 19th century by Brook Herford

'We doctors, in the treatment of nervous diseases, are now constantly compelled to prescribe periods of rest. Some periods are, I think, only Sundays in arrears.'

Sir James Crichton-Browne

'Sunday does not belong to business. It does not belong to the traders. It does not belong to industry. It does not belong to government . . . It belongs to God.'

Samuel Jeannes

Q. How should we as Christians treat Sundays?
Q. What sort of things should we do or not do?
Q. Can you apply this commandment to a non-Christian society?
Q. If you had to legislate about Sunday, what laws would you decide on?

13 Now what about forgiveness?

Wise Words

> God keeps no record of wrongs
> Jesus keeps no record of wrongs
> Love keeps no record of wrongs.
>
> 'I can forgive, but I cannot forget is only another way of saying I cannot forgive.'
>
> Henry Ward Beecher

Personal Survey:
Do you forgive
(a) always
(b) most times
(c) occasionally
(d) when I'm in the mood
(e) never

If you answered (b)—(e) then what things stop you from forgiving others? Is it when someone

(a) hurts you
(b) says an unkind word about you
(c) borrows something and does not return it
(d) makes a nuisance of themselves
(e) does not agree with you

If you ticked one or all of (a)—(f), then read on because you are in for a surprise because the Bible has got radical news about forgiveness.

Scripture Spotlight

Matthew 6: 12
'Forgive us our sins, just as we have forgiven those who have sinned against us.'

Matthew 6: 14
'Your heavenly father will forgive you if you forgive those who sin against you, but if you refuse to forgive them, he will not forgive you.'

Mark 11: 25
'But when you are praying, first forgive anyone you are holding a grudge against, so that your father in heaven will forgive you your sins too.'

Luke 6: 37
'Do not judge, and you will not be judged. Do not condemn, and you will not be condemned. Forgive, and you will be forgiven.'

Ephesians 4: 13
'Be kind to each other, tender hearted, forgiving one another, just as God has forgiven you because you belong to Christ.'

Colossians 3: 13
'Be gentle and ready to forgive, never hold grudges. Remember, the Lord forgave you, so you must forgive others.'

There are stacks more!

Before you go on . . .
If, in the Personal Survey, you ticked (e) then particularly look at Matthew 6: 14. If you ticked (d) then look again at Luke 6: 37. If you ticked (c) then look closely at Colossians 3: 13, and if you ticked (b) then look at Mark 11: 25.

We often talk about being Holy, being big for God and wonder what the secret is. The secret or secrets of the Christian Life are not in fact secret. They are lit up throughout the pages of the Bible and one of them (probably the main one) is simply to forgive others.

True repentance and a change of heart are essential for God's forgiveness, and if we really repent, then we will also forgive other people. But there are many people who will not forgive others. So what happens if we don't forgive those who have hurt us or said something unkind to us? One thing is clear and that is we will lose God's forgiveness. If I refuse to forgive other people, if I am hard towards other brothers and sisters, then God will not forgive me. In fact, if I do not forgive another person then I lose God's forgiveness, and in losing God's forgiveness I also lose my peace of mind. This does sound hard, but I honestly believe that it is things like this that hinder our growth and the furthering of God's Kingdom. I agree that Power evangelism and the Power of the Holy Spirit have their right place—what about forgiveness! Can you imagine if today every Christian forgave and sorted out any resentment or bitterness. What do you think would happen to the Church? You wouldn't have to ask for an outpouring of His Holy Spirit because we would all be filled with His Spirit.

There are many Christians today who have no peace of mind because they won't forgive someone else and because they won't forgive, they lay them-

selves open to trouble in mind, body and spirit. How many people today are becoming hard in face, becoming hard in outlook, and hard in character? The reason so often is because they won't forgive someone else. Many people are all snarled up inside, bitter and resentful. If I won't forgive another person, it reacts on me like a boomerang, and it hits me and can make me ill. As George Herbert once said: 'He who cannot forgive others breaks the bridge over which he must pass himself.'

Many Bible references are in the context of the Church family but what about 'Thou shalt love thy neighbour as thyself'—when your neighbour could include an enemy? How do we begin to forgive our enemies when we have enough problems forgiving those in our youth group or the Bible Study?

Everyone says forgiveness is a great idea until they have something to forgive! Then it's not such a good thing.

In Matthew 18: 21 – 35 we have the story of the unmerciful servant, which was a direct answer to Peter's question about forgiveness. 'Lord, how often shall my brother sin against me and I forgive him—until seven times?' What a wonderful suggestion that was from Peter.

The Rabbis, misinterpreting two chapters in the book of Amos, said that people were to be forgiven three times and no more, but Peter with the love of our Lord in his heart more than doubles the number and says 'seven times'.

Then Jesus says, 'No, Peter, you have still got it wrong; not seven times, but seventy times seven'—an infinite number of times (a lot!). And to press this truth home Jesus told the story of the unmerciful servant.

A certain man (v. 23) owed him ten thousand talents. Just to give you an idea how much that was,

Solomon's temple only cost nine thousand talents. It must have been the revenue for a whole province. This man lost the money (we don't know how), maybe through laziness, not bothering to collect the taxes. He may have been incompetent or perhaps he was totally dishonest and had embezzled the money. So, in accordance with the law of the land, the King gave orders that the man's possessions and goods were to be sold, and that together with his wife and family he was to be sold into slavery.

Verse 26 tells us that he fell on his knees and begged, 'I will pay back everything.' What a silly thing to say! He knew that he couldn't pay, that it was entirely beyond him. He could work until his dying day, but still never earn all that money to pay the King. In effect he threw himself completely at the King's mercy.

There is nothing whatever we can do to merit forgiveness. God will only grant us forgiveness out of His heart of compassion, His heart of love. And in the story the King did show mercy to the servant and forgave him despite all that he owed.

But when the servant went out he found someone who owed him little more than fifty pence, nothing in comparison to the debt that he owed to the King, and he took this man by the throat, would not grant him mercy, and cast him into prison. The story continues with the friends of the man thrown in prison telling the King about what had happened and, as a result, the King was furious at the servant's double standards and had him thrown into prison till he could repay.

You would have thought that the servant would have had more sense, but then that's exactly what so many of us do. God has forgiven us everything, so he tells us to forgive others.

Well, how do we forgive?

As a rule we tend to forgive others to the extent that we love God. The more God's love fills our lives the more forgiveness operates. It's simple, but the two are actually interlinked—so the more you try to forgive, that is to say, if you are wanting to, then God will give you the strength to do so . . . and then of course you enter into your own freedom in God's forgiveness and so are more blessed. If you find you can't forgive someone tell the Lord about it and ask Him to help you to do so. I know it is hard, but the joys are abundant if we do.

In writing this chapter I found that I was holding grudges against a member of my own church. I didn't realise I was, but the moment I realised, I felt uneasy. As soon as I forgave her in my heart and asked for God's love and forgiveness to enter my own life, I felt a new peace and joy. So if God has spoken to you through this—forgive and forget, and ask for God's healing to enter you, and ask God to bless that person.

A small boy, repeating the Lord's prayer one evening prayed: 'And forgive us our debts as we forgive those who are dead against us.' Amen!

Before you go—
Look at how Jesus forgave people. He was so filled with God's love he even forgave those who tortured Him and put Him to death—

'Two other men, both of them criminals, were also led out to be put to death with Jesus. When they came to the place called "The Skull", they crucified Jesus there, and the two criminals, one on His right and the other on His left. Jesus said,

110

"Forgive them, Father! They don't know what they are doing.'   Luke 23: 32 – 34

Have you ever seen such radical forgiveness?

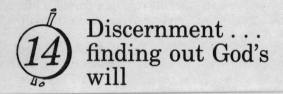

14 Discernment... finding out God's will

'So give your servant a discerning heart...' 1
Kings 3: 9

Discernment—getting to the mind of God, knowing
that He is speaking. I have been asked about this
more than any other question since I started travel-
ling six years ago. Discernment is the essential link
between Bible study, prayer and the active Christian life.

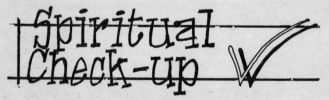

How do you discern what God is saying?
Well, it begins with us. First we must make sure
that:

1. We are wanting to do God's will. Unless it
really makes a difference to me what God

desires—unless I really want to do what He wants—discernment will be impossible. This is pretty tough but we must start here. We can hardly speak of being guided by God if God is unimportant or of minimum importance in our lives.

2. We are open to God. It is easy to say 'Yes', but God may play a significant role in a person's life, yet there may be no genuine desire to do His will. To be really open to God one must desire to do His will. All of us will find that our ideas of God can block us from discerning His voice as He speaks. This was the problem of the Pharisees with their view of Jesus. They were blinded by their own preconceptions. They were very religious, no doubt about that, but they sought God and their own ideas rather than God only.

Consider

1. Are we open to God?
2. Do we want 'God and' or 'God only'?
3. Do we have a knowledge of God? My faith must be based on solid knowledge of the person to whom I commit myself. If I don't know you, I can scarcely know what pleases you. Discernment of God's will depends a lot on our personal experience. The less personal experience I have of the Lord, the more I will have to depend on someone else. But the more you know God the more you will know what He wants you to do.

Recap

So are you looking for guidance? Then ask yourself:

(i) Are you a person who truly desires to accomplish God's work in the confused situations of life?

(ii) Are you open to be taught by and led by the Lord?

(iii) Do you know the Lord? Or are you getting to know the Lord, because obscure things can become clearer the more you get to know Him.

Married couples who have lived long together in love can often read between the lines; they are responsive to the smallest sign of what pleases or displeases the one they love. They can read in the eyes what has not been said in words.

An essential quality

'He leads the humble in the right way and teaches them His Will.' Psalm 25: 9

St. John of the Cross said that one of the surest signs of interior growth is a growing awareness of our own sinfulness, smallness and apparent weakness . . . what we would not expect. The Bible says that the simple understand God's word as it unfolds.

'The entrance of your words gives light, it gives understanding to the simple.' Psalm 119: 130

'. . . humility comes before honour.' Proverbs 18: 12

'. . . and with humility comes wisdom.' Proverbs 11: 2

Therefore the proud do not have true spiritual

wisdom. But the simple (not simple in mind!!) see what is right because they are ready to turn to God. They do no wrong and speak no lies (Zephaniah 3: 12 – 13).

But for the man who is wise in his own eyes there is little hope (Proverbs 26: 12). He is so sure of his thoughts and his ways that he cannot conceive that there is any other way. And he is more than a little confident that his thoughts and his ways are God's inspiration. The proud of course do not think of themselves as proud but mature. However, God chooses to guide the simple and honest and not the proud and arrogant. He listens to the humble, brings strength to their hearts and grants them a hearing (Psalm 10: 17).

Humility is both a preparation for the Holy Spirit and a result of the Holy Spirit. Now if we truly desire to do God's work, and are open to the Lord for His direction, spending time with Him and endeavouring to be as humble as we know how (if we are humble, we probably won't know) . . . then there is only one thing to add to this list and that is courage.

If a door is open, and we are doing all these things

that we've been talking about, then the open door is one that we need to have courage to go through. The Apostle Paul did not try to push open a closed door. He tried going through an open one, and no doubt prayed, as I have on many occasions, 'Please close that door, Lord if I'm on the wrong road!'

But of course it is not always plain sailing. There are occasions when a person is offered two jobs at the same time, when the advice of one friend differs from that of another; when the aspirations of a lifetime are swallowed up in the decision of a moment. We need then the still small voice of God. We need to hear God's voice saying

'This is the way, walk in it.'

This voice cannot be heard in the busyness of everyday life. The importance of getting alone with Him cannot be overstressed. Decisions which are to affect the whole of your life should be made with God in silence.

If there are still conflicting urges, the peace of God must 'be umpire'. The Lord always speaks in peace. Turmoil, anxiety and restlessness are not signs of His voice but of His absence from a situation.

If, however, all these factors have been taken into consideration and there is still uncertainty and ambiguity, speak to an older Christian; someone with more experience than you in the ways of the Lord; someone who is willing to journey with you to that point of discernment where prayer meets action. That's where nuns and monks are really useful. I go and see a monk once a month just to talk about things, and it has been a joy to seek, together with him, God's will when I am faced with decisions to make.

The important thing is that now you should persevere in the things we have talked about so that, as crossroad situations arise in the future, you will be, by the grace of God, a truly discerning person.

a prayer

Make me to know your ways, O Lord;
teach me your paths
Lead me in your truth, and teach me,
for you are the God of my salvation.

(15) Growing in discernment

Now, if a decision has already been made and you have, for example, got married, then do not question 'unchangeable' choices. Discerning God's will does not affect those areas. This comment may seem too obvious to be stated, but I have found that the Devil can make havoc for us by urging us to question repeatedly and worry about choices already made.

But what about where the choice was sincerely made and you now regret your decision and feel it was wrong? Well, the goodness of our God is perhaps most strikingly evident in His willingness to write straight with our crooked lines. He can draw the best out of our bad choices.

It does not mean we should make unwise or crooked choices simply because we will gain God's mercy. As Paul says in Romans 6, those who experience God's forgiving love in Christ Jesus can only desire to be confirmed more and more to this love in their own free choices.

If, however, decisions have been made before God that are now known to be wrong and are changeable, then don't worry about making that decision to change. However, if this is a big decision it would be wise to speak to an older Christian first.

How to discern what is right

1. Sometimes there is a revelation which is fairly rare. This is where the Lord moves in such a way that we know without hesitation. God's will is so clear that we cannot doubt what He wants. An example is Paul on the Damascus road when he was thrown off his horse, blinded and spoken to in a voice—

> 'I am Jesus, and you are persecuting me. Get up now and go into the city and you will be told what you have to do.'   Acts 9: 5

One day Jesus was walking by the customs house and he said to Matthew 'Follow me' and he got up and followed Him (Matthew 9: 9). Matthew's experience of God was so clear that he could not doubt who was speaking to him or what he wanted. In such cases of revelation there is no ambiguity, no uncertainty about God's will and so there really is nothing to discern. This is unlike the disciples John and Andrew who observed, questioned, 'came and saw', and only then made their discerning decision to remain with Jesus from that time onward (John 1: 35 – 39). This revelation route is not the usual way we discover the will of God.

2. Sometimes there is nothing, no overwhelming awareness of what God wants. Here God does not seem to be saying anything to us even though we are sincerely seeking His will. What would be helpful in this situation is to list the advantages and disadvantages of a decision. After you consider these, sense which is more reasonable. Sometimes the following three things can be helpful:

   (i) Consider the advice you would give if

someone came to you with the same
situation.
(ii) Imagine yourself which would you have
wished you had chosen.
(iii) Picture yourself standing in the presence of
God as judge and reflect what decision in
the present situation you would then wish
to have made.

In each case you will get some light on your present
circumstances which may be made clearer if you
distance yourself from them.

The rational weighing of the pros and cons and
the more imaginative way which has just been
explained can be effective in coming to a decision
when God seems to be leaving us to our natural
powers.

3. There is another way of discernment between
revelation and reasoning. That is when you have
come to some tentative choice rationally or through
the imagination methods described, and then give
the choice to the Lord for His confirmation. This is
what a lot of Christians do when faced with an
important decision and trying to figure out what
God wants. This is not wrong but it is not the
complete answer. Indeed we should bring our
decisions to the Lord to ask Him to confirm them,
but it is up to Him whether He confirms them or
not.

Discernment is always gradual and it is important
for you to believe that the Lord reveals His will step
by step. He does not give us a total, long-range
blueprint of His will for us. The Lord, it seems from
my limited experience, wants us to move ahead in
faith, to take the next step indicated, without seeing
clearly where it will ultimately lead. Often people

who ask my advice over an issue for which they
have sought God's guidance, want to know the final
outcome. 'If I apply to be a minister will I be
accepted?' 'If I am accepted will I be able to
persevere?' This is the desire that says 'I want to be
sure of the landing before I jump!'

Our Lord does not seem to want to work this way.
He reveals His will step by step and asks us to trust
our future to Him. For example, if you apply to a
college and you are not accepted that does not mean
that your well made discernment was a mistake.
If you made the best judgement you could with a
prayerful heart, the Lord is pleased. You only read
His will to some extent and the rest is up to Him.

Be aware of God in our feelings

Many of you will say at this point ... surely we

cannot trust our feelings. Well, I am assuming that we are practising everything in this book first!! Aren't feelings tricky and misleading? Is that not why we have been taught to make choices rationally and with a cool head? Yes, that is true but our feelings are crucial. To ignore them is to throw out the baby with the bath water. We must not be afraid of our feelings but we must seek God as to how we can distinguish the weeds from the wheat. If, for example, we have a growing sense of faith, hope, love, joy and worship, the common denominator is peace in the Lord. Or if we sense a lack of faith, hope and love we feel sad and separated from the Lord, here the common denominator is loss of God's peace. These two situations lead us to act, either to more prayer or a decision.

So the feelings are the raw material that we discern with. The mind judges the source and validity of these feelings and the will acts on the basis of this judgement.

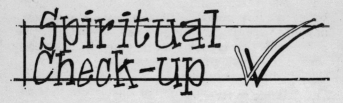

Spiritual Check-up

1   Are you desiring to do God's work?
2.   Are you open completely to Him?
3.   Do you know the Lord? So you are good friends?
4.   Are you humble in attitude?

If these four areas are a 'Yes' then consider

5.   Are you in touch with your feelings?

Begin to bring them to the Lord; ask Him to help you be in touch with them. To confirm a decision you rationally believe may be right through an inner peace or loss of peace. Number 5 takes time, so spend time with the Lord and don't get too hung up about it. When God told Noah to build an Ark, Noah was 600 years old!!

Scripture Spotlight

'In all your ways acknowledge Him and He will direct your paths.' Proverbs 3: 6

Making Decisions

When you are making significant decisions, how important are the following factors to you?

	Vital	Important	Not necessary
1. Talking to an older Christian	....	....	....
2. Seeing what the Bible might say	....	....	....
3. Thinking about the long-term effects	....	....	....
4. Deciding who might be personally affected by your choice	....	....	....

5. Spending time praying about it　　..... .. ..

6. Fasting about it　　..... .. ..

7. Seeking God's glory in the choice　　..... .. ..

8. Deciding the most sensible thing to do　　..... .. ..

9. Being peaceful about your choice　　..... .. ..

10. Asking God to bless the decision you are about to make　　..... .. ..

16 Natural evangelism

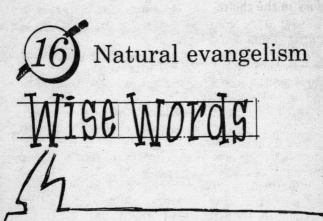

'A Christian is to be a keyhole through which other folk see God.'

Robert Gibson

'True Christianity is love in action.'

David McKay

'Christianity can be condensed into four words: Admit, Submit, Commit and Transmit.'

Samuel Wilberforce

'Christianity is like electricity: it cannot enter a person unless it can pass through.'

Richard Raines

'Christians should be like manure: not piled together in a smelly heap but scattered to fertilize and enrich.'

Anon.

Living for others

We have been filled with God's Holy Spirit, not to
stagnate like the Dead Sea without any outlet, but
to overflow to the benefit of others. As Christians it
is not so much that we have decided to follow Christ
but rather that He has chosen us and called us to
Himself and commissioned us with the task of
telling others about Him.

In the Cross we have a message that the World
cannot do without. Jesus Christ died for all the
world, so the world has a right to know about Him
and what He has done.

As Christians we should be informal 'mission-
aries'. We have to be witnesses. This word often
makes us feel uneasy and guilty; well, don't feel
that. Let's see how evangelism can become part of
our natural lifestyle and not a thing that is forced
or unnatural. A witness, as the Greek, word implies,
is a martyr. And the meaning of the word 'martyr'
is someone who witnesses to the truth.

Witnessing for Christ involves speaking for Him
and about Him; but, more than that, it also involves
being a living witness. We must witness by our lives
and our lips.

Being lights

'You are the light of the world.' Matthew 5: 14

The silent witness of a bright light in a dark place
speaks for itself. It is interesting to note that the
Greek word used here for light is the same as it
used for the fire or coals around which Peter stood
and warmed himself (Mark 14: 54). A fire is used
for heat more than for light. We must burn and

shine for all light comes from heat. We are called to be God's witnesses, a fire of coals to warm cold hearts, and lights to lighten the darkness of people's lives. Our daily lives must be the shining of Christ's radiant presence as we speak for Him. Also it is worth bearing in mind that to love to speak to people is one thing, but to love those to whom we speak is quite another. Only as we soak in the love of Christ can we really love others.

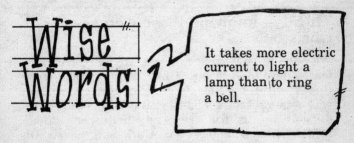

Wise Words

It takes more electric current to light a lamp than to ring a bell.

I have come across some Christians who don't think that it is necessary to tell others about God. All I can say is that some people obviously don't believe in telling others because they don't think what they believe is worth sharing!! There is no question about shining and telling others. It is how we do it that is the issue.

Witnessing with our lips for Jesus must be natural and spontaneous. The overflowing witness of a heart that cannot help but speak of that which it has experienced.

Here is a summary of what I think are the important steps for our effective 'telling others about Jesus'.

First—prayer

We need to pray for those around us that God may

indeed work in their lives and work through us. We need to be 'Strong in the Lord and in His mighty power'.   (Ephesians 6: 10)

Secondly—love and compassion

As we have already said, we need to love people—and love is the ultimate principle.

Thirdly—knowing those who are not Christians

We have to be with people who are not Christians for them to become Christians. Being with Christians all the time, in our Christian cliques, we will not be reaching non-Christians. It's really very difficult to catch fish in a pond where there are no fish! Jesus was amongst 'non-Christians' nearly all the time. But of course He never compromised Himself. He knew where to draw the line, and we must too. The place for a ship is in the sea, but God help the ship if the sea gets into it. So we must be amongst non-Christians, so long as we are good friends with the Lord, otherwise we might find that the world is having a greater effect on us than we are on it. Get involved in secular societies if you are at college, or get involved in local activities, sports clubs, local social action groups, welfare associations and so on. Move out!!

Fourthly—just be yourself

As we care for people they will soon see the difference in us. You don't have to set people up, like inviting your neighbours or friends round for coffee and saying, 'Do you like the coffee, and by the way what do you think of God?' It doesn't really flow. Be natural! Find out about them, and eventually they will ask 'You are different, why? What's happened to you?' Then, of course, you don't let such opportunities slip by. If you have built a good relationship with those you naturally come into contact with, like neighbours, colleagues and friends then, when you talk about God, they are faced with two options, either there is something wrong with you or you are right. But since they are your friends, they will no doubt believe that there is something in all this Christianity business. You may be the only Bible they ever read, so it could be good news or bad news. Let's pray and work at it being good news.

Fifthly—don't overfeed them

We don't feed babies with fish and chips! We have a tendency to over-feed. The moment we get an opportunity to speak about Christ we shove everything we know into them. No wonder they spew it up. There's no need to tell them everything at the first opportunity. Give them something to think about and let them chew it over, then they will come back for more.

Witnessing, evangelism, whatever it is called, is not just telling people to repent and accept Jesus as their Lord. It is caring, listening, which Jesus was so good at. Being a solid rock in a grumbling, hopeless, empty and lonely society—doing all this is also witnessing. Don't think that if you are not preaching out in the street that you are not witnessing. The most important thing is that witnessing becomes a part of your everyday life. If there are other opportunities that the Lord is prompting you to take—then that's a different situation.

I am an evangelist and in my work I travel miles to speak and tell people about Christ. But my wife and I still must be witnesses to friends and neighbours, so we invite them for dinner, to talk about anything. It soon comes out that we are different. After a while we sense that people want to know more. We started a group called 'The Day after Sunday Group' (it was on Monday night) and Justin Fashanu, Killy and I invited our friends to come for a twelve-week, once-a-week commitment, to look at what the Bible says on a variety of topics. We invited our hairdressers, neighbours, the owner of a restaurant. Ten people came . . . we had a fantastic time, a good meal, then discussion followed by coffee always at 10.00 p.m. . . . They never left till 12.00 p.m.!

We sowed seeds just through our natural contacts. Then we took a stop of faith in inviting them to a group, and to our amazement they came and we sowed more seeds. Now we sow the seeds and leave it to God to give the growth. So long as we sow seeds it doesn't matter. We often think if they don't become Christians then we are not sowing seeds properly. That's not the case. In our group some came to Christ and others did not. The important thing is that we keep in contact with all of them, whether they came to Christ or not. Where we failed in our group was that where the people did commit their lives to Christ we did not follow them up; we took them to Church and they found that difficult, and we didn't do anything—we should have started a nurture group.

Nurturing those who come to Christ is vital, as new babes in Christ are like lambs in a jungle of lions. So let's pray that we can tell others about Jesus. Not necessarily the powerful way (if God does, that's up to Him); not the spectacular way, or the aggressive way, but the *natural way;* if God calls *you* to do it in any other way, then do it.

⑰ Destination

Your destination as a Christian is heaven (big deal . . . I hear). A man had a small daughter who came home from Sunday School one day carrying a bundle of pamphlets. 'And what do you have here?' asked the father. 'Oh, nothing much,' answered the little girl. 'Just some ads. about heaven.' From what some people say it does seem as though people have got a bad impression of heaven. A teacher once said to a class of young children, 'Hands up those who want to go to heaven.' All the children put their hands up except one girl. 'Don't you want to go to heaven, Emily?' asked the teacher. 'No, not if that lot are going,' she replied. The teacher did not ask Emily where she would like to go.

Heaven is meant to be perfect happiness, pure bliss, joyful, delightful, ecstatic, but most Christians don't seem to be bubbling with real enthusiasm about going there.

Maybe the problem is because we have grown up with pictures and ideas of heaven that are not much when matched up to our modern, self-sufficient, technological world. Some pictures are of over-weight angels, well, at least fat-faced, wearing frilly night-clothes, floating around carrying miniature harps.

And then there is the classic statement—'When

132

you go to heaven you will see God.' This causes one of two reactions. Either: 'great, fantastic' or 'Oh, no. I'll cringe, knowing that He knows everything about me!'

So what does our Faith teach us about heaven?

A common question, particularly when, as Christians, we feel we are having a bad time and feel pretty battered, is . . . 'Is there really a heaven and, if God Almighty wants me to be happy for eternity, why am I having such a rough time down here?'

Jesus preached that we should store up treasure in heaven rather than on earth because, 'where your treasure is, there your heart will be also.' (Matthew 6: 21) Jesus *promised* that 'in My Father's house are many rooms; if it were not so, I would have told you. I am going there to prepare a place for you. And if I go and prepare a place for you, I will come back and take you to be with me that you also may be where I am.' (John 14: 2, 3)

And if you are feeling battered and rather low, then the verse just before this one says, 'Do not let your hearts be troubled. Trust in God; trust also in me.' These verses are in John 14 and the whole chapter deals largely with specific encouragements to counter-balance the departure of Jesus, the defection of Judas and the predicted failure of Peter. The encouragements are the ultimate provision of the Father's house, the return of Christ for His own, the prospect of doing greater works, unlimited prayer possibility, the gift of the Holy Spirit and the provision of Christ's peace. And if Peter, the leader amongst the disciples, was going to fail, it is no wonder hearts were troubled. Everything seemed on the verge of collapse. A renewed faith in God was necessary. The cause of Jesus seemed faced with defeat, so faith in Him was more needed than ever. Every fresh test as well as every new revelation is a summons to faith.

Jesus died on the Cross that we may enjoy His Presence in heaven. It cost Him His death so it must be some kind of a place if it cost Him that much to get us there. The phrase 'see God', in fact, can be quite misleading. A far better word is 'experience'. Really to experience God is fulness. Of course, at the moment, we can't handle everything that God says but He has given us a glimmer so that we can keep persevering and not flag nor give up. All the experiences you think are fantastic that you have ever had are just vague hints of what it will be like to experience God. Try and imagine your greatest experiences multiplied millions of times. Of course we can't quite grasp it, but this thought just gives an idea of what heaven will be like.

When we are risen with Him we will have brand new bodies (for those of you who have taken pills or insulin injections, Hallelujah, no more!). As for how God is going to do this, I don't know, but if God could create the universe and us to begin with, then He can handle this job easily enough. Even St. Paul says how foolish to ask this question (1 Corinithians 15:35). What we do know is that it is going to happen and that our resurrected bodies will be different.

Heaven, yes it is true, we don't know much about it, but we do know it's real, and that's where we are heading. So keep your eyes fixed on Jesus in heaven, but don't be so heavenly minded that you are of no earthly use, as someone said.

Be *determined*

'No eye has seen
No ear has heard
No mind has conceived
What God has prepared for those who love Him.'

1 Corinthians 2: 9

AMEN!

Wise Words

'Heaven would hardly be heaven if we could define it'

William Biederwolf

'Heaven is the presence of God'

Christina Rossetti

'Anyone can devise a plan by which good people may go to heaven. Only God can devise a plan whereby sinners, who are His enemies, can go to heaven.'

Lewis Chafer

'In heaven, to be even the least is a great thing, where all will be great; for all shall be called the children of God.'

Thomas à Kempis

'Go for it'

Modern twentieth century proverb

Recommended reading

The Great Divorce by C. S. Lewis